This is the kind of book I like to

I like its style and the way it communicates truth through the ...
word.

I believe it will practically help many people to understand and walk in God's ways concerning Kingdom finances.

Even though Chris covers some controversial subjects, I believe this book is balanced and has the potential to straighten out people's hearts with understanding. It will bring them into a place of trusting and believing God with their finances.

This book will show them how to live the truth they believe, as a way of life in Christ.

Cecil H Paxton – Cecil and Lisa Paxton Ministries Inc

Rejecting **Mammon**

How to See Results From Your Giving

Chris **Cree**

REJECTING MAMMON: How to See Results From Your Giving

Copyright © 2019 by Chris Cree

All rights reserved.

Published by SuccessCREEations, LLC

To my wife Lisa.
Thank you for partnering with me on this great adventure.
You know just how to add the right touch of joy and fun to every day.

And to everyone who is frustrated, waiting to see the harvest from all your faithful giving. Please take hope in the knowledge that God does have answers for you. Your harvest is fast approaching and it will fuel a cycle of seedtime and harvest which will propel you into an even deeper relationship with Jesus.

CONTENTS

Introduction

"Ask, and it will be given you. Seek, and you will find. Knock, and it will be opened for you."
— Matthew 7:7 (WEB)

Why This Book?

There's something about the subject of money that gets people's emotions all stirred up. People react passionately, and often negatively, when Christian ministers start talking about money.

For example, a sure way to kick over an anthill in Christian circles on Facebook is to post something about tithing. People tend to get irrational and lash out when their views about money are challenged.

I totally get it. I've seen manipulative ministers apply emotional and spiritual pressure to get people to put more money in the plate when they "take up" offerings. Unfortunately it happens far more than it should.

For my part, I dislike talking about money more than most people. I don't have a good sense of what things are worth. And I really don't like rejection. That combination made for epic failures the few times I tried my hand at sales jobs.

All in all, I'd rather write a book about something else.

However, I keep running into people with questions about giving. It seems like at least once a week I hear someone ask a question about giving and money. Or I see a question on social media and my heart goes out to the person.

- *Should we give 10% today, or what's in our heart to give?*

- *Is the tithe relevant for believers today?*

- *How come I have been giving faithfully for years, but never seem to harvest much?*

- *Why is there so much manipulation and fear surrounding money?*

- *Didn't Jesus say we shouldn't talk about our giving and not even let our right hand know what our left hand is doing?*

- *What's the deal with the thirty, sixty, hundredfold harvest and why don't we see that?*

- *Since the tithe is part of the Law, then shouldn't we disregard it today?*

- *How come I don't see any results from my giving?*

I had all these questions and many more myself. So I know that even though it makes people crazy sometimes to talk about money, this is the right book for me to publish right now.

God truly does have answers to all our questions, even the tough ones about money. The Kingdom of God provides ways for us to prosper in every area of our lives, including financially. Jesus said that money is the least thing when it comes to exercising our faith. He said that if we weren't faithful with money, then who will trust us with true riches?

I believe it is time for the Church of Jesus Christ to rise up and step into the prosperity He already made available for us. When we finally get a revelation of this and begin to receive the fullness of His financial prosperity the way God intends, it will change everything, both for us personally, and for the world around us.

Once we understand how to receive from God in the area of our finances, it unlocks the door to receive His blessings in every other area of our lives too because money is the least thing in the Kingdom. And it will empower you to become a greater influence for the Kingdom of God in your world as you demonstrate your faithfulness in giving and receiving and come to understand God's intended purpose behind the prosperity He gives you.

Where We've Been

This book is the result of years of both study and practical experience.

For the first fifteen or so years of our marriage my wife Lisa and I tended to have what I generally refer to as "intense fellowships." No matter how much I try to be funny or make it sound more spiritual, the reality for those years is that we argued quite a bit.

Somehow money seemed to be at the core of at least 99% of those arguments. If you're married, perhaps you can relate to arguing about money. Or if you're single, perhaps you worry about money issues. For us, far too often there was too much month at the end of our money. Lisa did the books. She couldn't see how to make it work when there wasn't enough to pay the bills. I didn't really have any answers for her. And since I didn't like talking about money anyway, I just avoided the subject as long as possible.

The pressure would build and at some point the lid would blow off. When it did, I got angry and loud. Then she cried. Or sometimes she cried and then I got angry and loud. Either way I felt incompetent, like I was a horrible provider. But because I was better with words I would get her all twisted around. Then she would feel defeated.

We both felt powerless and hopeless to see things change.

It got to the point where we called it the crazy cycle because even when we were fully aware of what was happening, that we were "going there" one more time, we still went there anyway. Over, and over, and over again.

One day we had a particularly bad "intense fellowship" and Lisa got so angry that she kicked a chair over. It shocked my system.

Standing there, in that moment, I felt like a total failure as a husband, because I was sure it was my fault. I was the one to blame for our financial challenges and the strain it caused in our relationship.

And I felt like a total failure as a Christian too. Following Jesus is supposed to make our lives different. But I couldn't even figure out how to stop arguing about money with my own wife.

Fortunately our story doesn't end there. We knew there had to be answers.

There were many reasons why Lisa and I decided to attend Bible college. One of the biggest is that we both clearly saw how desperately we needed to renew our minds and break the crazy cycle.

In reality we both had very different, but very dysfunctional thinking and attitudes towards money. Bible college helped us dramatically as we learned what all Jesus accomplished for us on the cross.

But we still had a problem. Even though we got a revelation that we now *are* prosperous in Christ, we still didn't know *how* to prosper. There was a disconnect because the prosperity that we knew was ours wasn't part of our practical experience. We knew the truth of prosperity, but we didn't yet see it playing out in our lives.

We were always really good at giving. But we didn't know how to receive. We had been faithfully sowing financial seed for years and years. But we didn't know how to harvest. We were just giving, giving, giving in ignorance, not realizing that God has explained specific ways for us to give in His Kingdom. God's ways are higher than our ways.

This disconnect became glaringly obvious after God called us to head overseas as missionaries. We needed to raise financial support to get where God was calling us so we put all the pieces in place.

We formed a nonprofit and got the 501(c)3 approval. I built a website and put up a secure giving form. We started an email newsletter. And we prayed.

But the money we needed just trickled in.

At the slow rate we were receiving donations it was going to take us decades to raise what we needed to cover our living expenses. The only method of fund raising we were exposed to required us to itinerate at a bunch of churches and ask people to support us.

Unfortunately we didn't really have any church contacts where we could go speak. Even more, the thought of traveling around to churches begging for money didn't appeal to us at all. We very much didn't want to do that. But we didn't know any other way.

It was during this time that God told me, *"Chris, I want you to stop working for your money and start believing for it."*

I objected. Have you ever done that? Have God tell you something, then try to explain to Him why what He said isn't right? I took God right back to His own word in 2 Thessalonians 3:10 where Paul wrote that if anyone doesn't work, then neither should he eat.

I figure if I'm going to argue with God, then I better use His own words to argue my side.

God pointed out that He didn't say I should stop working. He said I was to stop working *for my money.* He wanted me to disconnect the results from my own effort.

That was a mind bender for me. It took some time to get my head around it. The skills I had always enabled me to earn pretty good money. We didn't realize it at the time, but God was going to show Lisa and me how His Kingdom works in the area of our finances. That meant He needed me to disconnect from my old way of getting provision through my hard work.

We dug into scripture. We sought out more teaching and found mentors who helped us. We tested what we learned to see what bore fruit and what didn't. We started putting what we learned into practice, and we saw results. People started donating to our ministry without us begging them.

It was much less than a year from when we began aligning our giving with the ways of the Kingdom of God that the funds we needed were in place. Lisa and I moved to Scotland, where God called us to open a new campus of an international Bible college.

The money we needed to carry out God's assignment came in supernaturally, much faster than the decades it would have taken in the natural. This book will show you what that looks like.

I first pulled this material together as a course which I teach to our Bible college students. They are seeing results just like Lisa and I do. God is no respecter of persons. His Kingdom principles work for anyone who will line up with them. His promises are available for everyone who will believe them and receive them by faith.

God will do the same thing for you too. His promises are there, waiting for you to believe them and receive them by faith. There's lots of work to do before Jesus returns. It's going to take a great deal of money to get it all done.

It is God's desire that you become a financial resource for His Kingdom. But you cannot give away what you don't yet have. Therefore we must leave the world's ways of prospering financially behind and start walking in God's ways instead.

It's my prayer that this book will reveal those Kingdom ways in the area of your finances and help you step into the prosperity God has waiting for you. That will enable you to bless even more people than you do already.

> *And God is able to make all grace abound toward you, that you, always having all sufficiency in all things, may have an abundance for every good work.* — 2 Corinthians 9:8 (NKJV)

Chapter 1

A Tale of Two Systems

"No one can serve two masters, for either he will hate the one and love the other; or else he will be devoted to one and despise the other. You can't serve both God and Mammon."
— Matthew 6:24 (WEB)

Heavenly Access Point

Your heart follows your wallet. So does mine.

That makes it shockingly easy to determine what we really value. All we need to do is look at our credit card statements, checkbooks, and bank accounts. They will be a more accurate indication of the priorities of our heart than any test we could take.

Jesus knew this and said as much. His desire is for us to experience as much of the Kingdom of Heaven in our own lives right now as possible. That's why He told us to give our money toward Kingdom purposes and causes, to things with eternal significance. He knew our heart follows our money.

But don't take my word for it. Look at what Jesus said,

"Do not be afraid, little flock, for it is your Father's good pleasure to give you the kingdom. Sell your possessions and give alms. Provide yourselves purses that do not grow old, an unfailing treasure in the heavens, where no thief comes near and no moth destroys. For where your treasure is, there will your heart be also." — Luke 12:32-34 (MEV)

It's interesting that Jesus starts out by telling us not to be afraid. Why would He do that?

The reason Jesus tells us not to be afraid is because He says something next that is frightening to our hearts. Let's be honest. Giving what you have away goes against everything we were trained in by the world system we knew before we became a believer.

The truth is, you're kidding yourself if you think you can experience the best of the Kingdom without giving money into it, or by only giving a token amount when the offering plate passes by.

Jesus did not say your wallet follows your heart. Your treasure leads. Your heart follows.

Even something as simple and basic as the previous paragraph will rub some people the wrong way. Jesus is saying that you can have as many wonderful thoughts about God's ways of doing things as you want. But until you give your own money into the Kingdom, your heart will never really be in it.

Not only that, but your heart will be in the Kingdom to the degree that you choose to give your finances into it. You are not buying holiness or favor with God. Instead, your giving reveals how passionate your heart is for the things of God, plain and simple.

Notice what Jesus says happens when we give away what we have. He says doing so provides purses for ourselves. Your purse, or in my case my wallet, is the access point to your estate. Now your estate may not be very big. Or it may be huge. But if you're like me your wallet has some sort of identification, perhaps your driver license. I also keep my bank cards in my wallet too. With these things in my wallet I can access all the financial resources that are available to me. That's how I access my provision as I go about my day.

And that's exactly what Jesus says our giving provides for us in God's Kingdom. Giving is the access point for us to connect with the abundance and provision of Heaven. It's the gateway through which we bring Kingdom prosperity into our lives here and now.

The Kingdom of God

Ultimately this is all about the Kingdom of God because that is what the Gospel of Jesus is all about.

The Gospel of Jesus Christ is good news. And it turns out it is very specific good news. Jesus said it's the good news of the Kingdom of God.

We see this in scripture. The word "gospel" appears 110 times in the New King James Version of the New Testament.

In his letters, Paul mentions the word gospel more than any other New Testment writer, at 79 times:

- Gospel of the grace of God (x1)

- Gospel of the glory of Christ (x1)

- Gospel of your salvation (x1)

- Gospel of peace (x2)

- Mostly: Gospel of God, or Gospel of Christ, or just the word Gospel (93%)

Since the overwhelming majority of the times Paul mentions the word Gospel, he refers to Jesus, that means we need to look at what Jesus said His good news was about.

When we read through Matthew, Mark, Luke, and John with an eye to see, it becomes obvious that Jesus said it is the Gospel of the Kingdom of God.

For example, in Luke Jesus was talking about John the Baptist when He said this,

> *The law and the prophets were until John. Since that time the kingdom of God has been preached, and everyone is pressing into it.*
> — Luke 16:16 (NKJV)

There Jesus says that the Kingdom of God is the replacement for the Old Testament law and prophets.

In Matthew chapter 24 Jesus is talking about the end times when he says this,

> *And this gospel of the kingdom will be preached in all the world as a witness to all the nations, and then the end will come.* — Matthew 24:14 (NKJV)

There Jesus clearly calls it the "gospel of the kingdom." He said that is the gospel which will be preached until the end of time. In another passage, Jesus says that preaching the Kingdom of God is the reason He was sent here.

> *But He said to them, "I must preach the kingdom of God to the other cities also, because for this purpose I have been sent."* — Luke 4:43 (NKJV)

According to Jesus, the Kingdom of God is the very good news He was sent down here on earth to preach. Preaching the Kingdom was his self-declared purpose.

How would you describe the Kingdom of God?

The simplest way to say it is that the Kingdom of God is God's way of doing things. And we know that God's ways are not our ways, right?

> *For My thoughts are not your thoughts,*
> *Nor are your ways My ways," says the Lord.*
> *"For as the heavens are higher than the earth,*
> *So are My ways higher than your ways,*
> *And My thoughts than your thoughts.* — Isaiah 55:8-9 (NKJV)

God has a way of doing things that is very different than man's worldly way of doing them. In the world's way of doing things, the strong dominate the weak, and the rich oppress the poor.

But the Kingdom of God is different. In the Kingdom of God, the strong defend the weak, and the wealthy bless the poor. The Kingdom of God is designed so that everyone can prosper. God is all about creating situations and circumstances where everyone wins.

The Kingdom of God is about making a world that works for everyone and leaves no one out. I've heard it referred to as, "systems for human flourishing."

That's why I call this chapter A Tale of Two Systems. I simply use the word "system" to mean "way of doing things." We are going to compare the system of the world that we are all familiar with against the system of the Kingdom of God in the area of finances. It's a comparison between God's ways and the world's ways where finances and provision are concerned. We're going to find out that the two systems use very different approaches and therefore produce very different results.

Here's something to think about,

Your system is perfectly structured to produce the results you are seeing.

If you don't like the results you see, then something needs to change in your system. You need to adjust the way you do things.

And since the Kingdom of God is a righteous and just system, then it must work the same for you as it does for me, right? It must work the same for the preacher on TV too as it does for us.

Well that's what Lisa and I ran into when we began preparing to move overseas on the mission field. There was something wrong with our system. Our ways were not lined up with God's ways of doing things. Therefore we weren't seeing the prosperity we knew the Bible clearly says has been supplied for us as believers in Jesus and children of God.

We weren't getting the results that we knew we should have. That meant that there was something wrong on our end, because whatever was going on was perfectly structured to produce the results we were getting.

We needed to change our system — change our thinking, get

revelation in the area of finances, and line up with God's ways of doing things, so that we could see the Kingdom of God work in this area. Something needed to change for us to get to our assignment in Scotland.

The more we study this, the more we realize how vitally important what I'm sharing with you in this book is. Once you get a revelation about how these two systems work — about how the world's system works compared to how the Kingdom of God's system works — you cannot "unsee" it.

The more we look at it, the more we realize it's *everywhere*.

Money Touches Everything

Money touches everything in our world. There may have been a time when folks could survive without ever touching money. Perhaps it was possible at some point in the past for people to do just fine bartering what they were able to produce for the things they needed to get by in life.

But those days are long gone.

Today, money and some level of contact with it is a hard requirement even for basic survival in life.

Think about it. Every single thing you touched since you woke up this morning was paid for by someone, somewhere, with money.

You must come to an understanding of this. Without money ministry simply does not happen. In order to have a place for a church to meet, it takes money. Buildings have to be leased or purchased, utilities, furniture, and equipment paid for.

If you are called to a traveling ministry, transportation, hotel accommodation, food — pretty much everything — costs money.

Our finances were important to Jesus. He certainly talked about money and finances a whole bunch. Several of his parables are specifically about money and how we relate to our finances.

Then on top of that are all the other scriptures that address finances and provision from the Law, Proverbs and Psalms, the Prophets, and the various New Testament epistles. It's incredibly obvious that God has a great deal to say about money, finances, and provision.

Epic Battle of the Ages

The truth of the matter is that we're in a war, and not just any war. It is the ultimate struggle of Good and Evil on the grandest scale possible.

We're talking Narnia. Fortunately we're on Aslan's side and we know he will save the day in the end. I mean just read the book of Revelation and you'll see.

It's not unlike the Lord of the Rings where we stand beside the rightful king to stop the evil overlord Sauron and his massive orcish army.

We're the ragtag rebel alliance in a desperate fight against the well equipped and the seemingly overwhelming resources of the evil galactic empire.

Only we shouldn't be ragtag. We shouldn't be undersupplied and ill-equipped. Somewhere along the way we bought into a lie. Somehow we think that Jesus commissioned us to go and create disciples of the whole earth without providing the resources that it takes to get the task done.

We misread scripture. Let me give you an example. Go to 2 Timothy 3:16,

> *All Scripture is given by inspiration of God, and is profitable for doctrine, for reproof, for correction, for instruction in righteousness, that the man of God may be complete, thoroughly equipped for every good work.*

Unfortunately, many Christians read the words in that passage as written, yet their brains instead interpret it something like this: "All Scripture, except those passages that relate to money, is given by inspiration of God, and is profitable for doctrine, for reproof, for correction, for instruction in righteousness, that the man of God may be continually in need, partially equipped just for those good works that don't require any resources in the natural."

Now I get that we are spiritually equipped for every good work. The equipping absolutely is spiritual. However, the passage says we are *thoroughly* equipped. That means we are equipped in the spiritual *and* in the natural for the work God has for us in this life.

All Scripture is given by inspiration of God, including those passages that relate to money.

Jesus gave us a mission: Go and make disciples of all nations. He taught us how to pray: *"Our Father which art in heaven, Hallowed be thy name. Thy kingdom come. Thy will be done in earth, as it is in heaven...."* — Matthew 6:9-10 (KJV)

Thy will be done in earth, as it is in heaven. It's going to take some financial resources to bring God's will to our hurting world.

God offered Lisa and me an assignment: Disciple people in Scotland to grow in the ways of the Kingdom of God, to literally bring the Kingdom of God to earth here in Scotland. We've been invited into His mission to go and make disciples of all nations.

That's a God-sized assignment! One of the primary tools He's given me and Lisa to accomplish our part in the task is the Bible college campus we head up today here in Scotland.

Here are just some of the tangible, natural, dare I say worldly, things that are required for us to accomplish what God Himself has put in front of us to do:

- Plane tickets

- Visas

- Housing

- Furnishings in the housing

- Food

- A Car

- Marketing to reach potential students

- A building for the school to meet in

- Furnishings for the school

- Utilities

- Staff

And the list goes on. Someone somehow had to pay for all that stuff.

Fortunately, Lisa and I are learning what Paul told the church in Philippi who gave to him financially in spite of their poverty: *And my God shall supply all your need according to His riches in glory by Christ Jesus.* — Philippians 4:19 (NKJV)

Financial Principles

Far too many people are believing God for financial increase and prosperity, while at the same time regularly violating the very financial principles laid out in all those scriptures. You may be a mighty man or woman of God. But if you jump off a cliff you are still going to get smacked in the face by the reality of the law of gravity as you fall to the rocks below.

When it comes to finances you cannot regularly violate basic Kingdom financial principles and then expect God to continually show up with miracles to bring increase. That path only leads to frustration.

God will not go back on His word.

> *My covenant I will not break, nor alter the word that has gone out of My lips.* — Psalms 89:34 (NKJV)

The reason God will not go back on His word is because He cannot lie (see Titus 1:2).

Because the Bible thoroughly explains how finances work in the Kingdom of God, that means violating those principles and laws, or trying to do things a different way than God reveals in His word, will hinder you from seeing Kingdom results in your finances.

When we choose to use financial ways that are different than the ways of God that He set up for His Kingdom to operate with, then we will get different results. It really is that simple.

It Won't Fall In Our Laps

Many of these folks who don't understand what the Bible has to say about money are sitting back waiting for financial prosperity to fall in their laps. It doesn't work that way.

For one thing there isn't any money in Heaven. Think about it. We're talking about a place that uses gold as paving material for its streets. Nowhere in Scripture does it say that there is any cash in Heaven.

Money is an invention of man designed to work in the worldly economic system of buying and selling. In contrast the Kingdom of God uses a different economic system of giving and receiving. Money is a product of this world, not heaven.

The next time you take a note out of your wallet or purse look at it. It says right on it who it belongs to. Generally speaking it will be the central bank of the country which produced it. In the USA all our currency says Federal Reserve Bank on it, because they're the ones who mint the currency.

Here in the Scotland the Bank of England designates three banks:

- Bank of Scotland

- Royal Bank of Scotland

- Clydesdale Bank

None of us have any currency in our possession that says, "Bank of Heaven" on it.

So believers who are sitting around expecting God to drop a pile of money in their laps are confused. That's a long wait for a train that won't come. If God did that, they would be counterfeit bills. Obviously God is not a counterfeiter.

At the same time God absolutely will bring resources to us so we can accomplish the Kingdom purposes he puts in our hearts. But God moves those resources to us in the natural through people. God provides for us supernaturally, but He usually does so through natural means.

Think about our case and that list of things we need to accomplish our mission here in Scotland. Every one of those things was provided for us by God. And every one of them has come to us through people.

Some of those people are our ministry partners who commit some of their finances to be a part of what God is doing. Some of the items will be provided through the student tuition fees. Other things are provided by the parent ministry for the Bible College here in the UK.

And then there are non-cash contributions. For example God spoke to an English couple who gave Lisa and me the first car we owned when we arrived here.

But one way or another all of those resources have come to us in the natural through other people. God provides for his people through other people. It's all about participating in the Kingdom of God.

So let's take a look at that.

Mammon

Jesus says something very profound to us in Matthew 6:24,

> *No one can serve two masters; for either he will hate the one and love the other, or else he will be loyal to the one and despise the other. You cannot serve God and mammon.*

You might see a slightly different word used at the end of that verse depending on the translation you have. Some Bibles have that last sentence saying, "You cannot serve God and money."

I call that an unfortunate translation because it creates confusion rather than making the verse more easily understood.

Let's look at that word "mammon". It's actually the Aramaic word *mammōnas*. It only occurs here in Matthew and then Jesus uses it three times in Luke chapter 16, which we'll look at in a little bit. This verse in Matthew is basically a duplicate of one of those times it's used in Luke.

Yet Jesus talked about money a whole bunch of other times where he used different words.

Sometimes Jesus spoke about a specific coin like he did in Matthew 17:27. If you remember the story, that's when Jesus told Peter where the money to pay their taxes was hidden. He said Peter should go fishing and look in the mouth of the first fish he caught. There Jesus said, "you will find a piece of *money*."

In that case it is the Greek word *statēr*, which was a specific coin of that day that happened to be valued at exactly twice the amount of the temple tax. Therefore Peter could pay the tax for himself and for Jesus with that one coin.

Another time Jesus referred to coins in general like with Matthew 22:19.

In that passage, the Pharisees and Herodians set a trap for Jesus when they asked Him about paying the Roman tax. They knew if Jesus said to pay the tax the Jews wouldn't like it. But if He said not to pay the tax, then that would cause problems with the Roman authorities.

In response to their question, Jesus said, "Show me the tax *money*."

There Jesus used the Greek word *nomisma*, which was a general word for money when referring coins or legal tender.

Then in Matthew 25 Jesus tells the parable of the talents. In verse 18 He refers to money with yet another Greek word when He says, "But he who had received one went and dug in the ground, and hid his lord's *money*."

That's the Greek word *argyrion*, which refers to a silver piece or a shekel.

Now call me old fashioned if you like. But I believe that Jesus was intentional about what words he used. If Jesus meant to say that we cannot serve God and "money" then He had a variety of Greek words to choose from to say that.

Instead Jesus used a particular Aramaic word. In Jesus' day that Aramaic word mammon referred to a Syrian god of riches. Originally the word came from ancient Chaldea, which is Babylon.

Do you remember how Babylon got its name?

The first time we see it mentioned is in Genesis chapter 11 with the Tower of Babel.

> *Therefore its name is called Babel, because there the Lord confused the language of all the earth; and from there the Lord scattered them abroad over the face of all the earth.* — Genesis 11:9 (NKJV)

In the King James, that Hebrew word is translated Babylon 257 times and is rendered Babel only twice, once here and once in Genesis chapter 10. It's the same word for both.

Do you know how tall the Tower of Babel was? According to my research, the experts say it was 300 feet tall. I have no idea how they determined that height.

How tall is the tallest manmade structure today? As of this writing, the tallest building is 2,722 feet tall! The Burj Khalifa in Dubai and was opened in 2010. In comparison, the tallest building in the European Union is the Shard in London at 1,016 feet, less than half as high. The tallest building in the United States as of this writing is One World Trade Center in New York City at 1,776 feet, which is also the year America was founded.

All that to say, based on the fact that we have man made structures 9 times higher than the tower of Babel, I think it's safe to conclude that the fact that they were building a tall tower wasn't the actual problem.

This verse points us in the direction of the problem,

> *And they said, "Come, let us build ourselves a city, and a tower whose top is in the heavens; let us make a name for ourselves, lest we*

be scattered abroad over the face of the whole earth." — Genesis 11:4
(NKJV)

Then Isaiah sheds a little more light on the problem with the Tower of
Babel for us,

> *How you are fallen from heaven,*
> *O Lucifer, son of the morning!*
> *How you are cut down to the ground,*
> *You who weakened the nations!*
> *For you have said in your heart:*
> *'I will ascend into heaven,*
> *I will exalt my throne above the stars of God;*
> *I will also sit on the mount of the congregation*
> *On the farthest sides of the north;*
> *I will ascend above the heights of the clouds,*
> *I will be like the Most High.'* — Isaiah 14:12-14 (NKJV)

The problem was that mankind wanted to make a name for themselves
and take God's place.

Take a look at this quote I found on the Wikipedia page for the
building in Dubai: *"The decision to build the building is reportedly based on
the government's decision to diversify from an oil-based economy, and for
Dubai to gain international recognition."*

Isn't it interesting that the motivation for building that tower in Dubai
was economic and to make a name for themselves. Not much has
changed about human nature in the 4-5,000 years since the tower of
Babel!

Let's take a moment to review what we have at this point.

We know that Jesus deliberately used a different word from the
generic word for money or any of the other Greek words that refer to
money when he said we cannot server God and mammon.

We know that the word mammon refers to a god of riches whose roots
go all the way back to ancient Babylon.

And we also know that the same ungodly impulses that motivated the
people to build the tower of Babel at the founding of ancient Babylon

are still motivating people today. These impulses actually line up with those of Satan rather than God.

Spirit of Antichrist

Let me ask you a question. Today, what do we call something that sets itself up in opposition to God? We call that antichrist.

At its core mammon is ultimately the spirit of antichrist.

How do we know this?

We can look to the mark of the beast in the book of Revelation,

> *and that no one may buy or sell except one who has the mark or the name of the beast, or the number of his name.* — Revelation 13:17 (NKJV)

The antichrist threat which mammon powers, is that money is the answer to all our problems. Mammon says that money is our source instead of God.

Mammon uses access to money as a means for:

- Intimidation

- Manipulation

- Control

The Kingdom of God uses money to set captives free, bless people, and expand the Kingdom.

Mammon is anchored in **Scarcity**. There is never enough within the mammon system. Therefore I must selfishly hoard because once I run out of what I have, I will suffer lack.

In contrast, the Kingdom of God is floating in **Abundance**. Within the ways of the Kingdom of God, you can be generous and give freely because God is your source and He will return what you give away and more!

As an analogy, we can think of the two contrasting systems being represented by two different kinds of pie. I like pie. (Who doesn't like pie?)

The world operates with the mammon pie you are probably accustomed to seeing. That pie is limited. In that system, if I take a slice of pie, then it leaves that much less pie for you to potentially enjoy. Once a slice of pie is taken from the mammon system, it limits how much pie is available for everyone else. In the mammon system, pie is a purely natural and limited resource so decisions are made based on its scarcity.

The Kingdom of God is different because instead of being anchored in scarcity it's floating in abundance. The Kingdom pie is like an ever expanding and unlimited pie. That means the amount of pie you enjoy has absolutely no impact on how much pie I can receive. You can have as much pie as you want in the Kingdom because, even if you completely stuff your belly with all the pie you could possibly eat, it in no way limits how much pie God can make available for me to receive.

In the Kingdom of God, pie is supernatural and unlimited.

Remember, this is an analogy. So please don't write me asking for the recipe for Kingdom pie!

I should also point out that mammon is driven by **Fear of Loss**. Because mammon is anchored in scarcity, it opens the door for fear to come in. Even when someone has plenty in the mammon system, they really can't enjoy it because there is an ever present fear that they will lose what they have.

In contrast, the Kingdom of God is propelled by the **Blessings of God** because it is floating in God's abundance. The blessings of God are powerful. Think about it.

Most people understand curses pretty easily. They see that if someone is cursed they can do everything right and still get a bad result because they are cursed.

What can be more difficult for believers to get their heads around is that the opposite is true too. When someone is under the blessings of God, even if they do everything wrong, they will still see a good result anyway.

And the really good news is this. God's blessings are far more powerful than any curse the enemy can put on you. As a believer in Jesus those blessings already belong to you. It's just a case of you believing it and receiving them.

Examples of Mammon

Let me give you a few examples of what mammon looks like when it is operating in the world.

Here in the UK they have a lot of commercials for charities on the TV. We see them in the States too. You know the ones I mean. They show images designed to pull hard on your emotions, usually of suffering children or animals. The celebrity announcer recounts a horribly sad story describing the suffering in graphic detail. All the while the music playing in the background strikes just the desired sad notes.

The whole thing is designed to manipulate your emotions so that you pick up the phone right then, call in, and make a donation.

Commercials like that are tapping into the mammon system to emotionally manipulate you into giving the charity money.

If you are afraid of losing your job, that is mammon putting fear of loss on you to control you. Believe it or not, you don't get extra points in the Kingdom of God for worrying.

When you already fear losing your job, it's very possible mammon will crank up the pressure by attempting to get you to compromise your values. If you are not aware of the spiritual forces at work, you won't realize that this fear creates a perpetual cycle. The more you are motivated by fear to compromise, the more fearful you will become. With each new compromise you sacrifice another piece of your soul.

The only escape from that trap is trusting God and recognizing that He is the true source of your provision and not your job. The job just happens to be the channel through which He is flowing that provision today. Until you shift into a place where you know that if that job goes away, God will still provide for your needs some other way, you will stay under mammon's control in your work.

Some people look to debt as their primary way to solve financial challenges instead of trusting God to supply their needs. When the default answer to any financial challenge is to put it on the credit card, or get another loan, then that is mammon digging its hooks deeper into you.

Proverbs says the borrower is the slave of the lender (Proverbs 22:7). If debt is the primary way you look to solve your financial problems, then that should be a warning to you that you are under mammon's control. It shows that you have a slave mentality and don't yet fully appreciate your full true identity as a son or daughter of God and heir to the whole estate.

When you see sales pitches that use false scarcity like "only 3 left" or "today only" as artificial ways to drive more sales, that is a mammon influenced sales process.

People who give or withhold money as a means to manipulate or control others are aligning with mammon.

Believers who let their bank accounts determine when and how they follow the will of God are under mammon's influence. One of the joys of living in the Kingdom of God is that we have the liberty to follow God's leading including His timing because the provision that obedience requires is already in place.

Another example I've come across is instances where I've seen people refuse the offer of supernatural healing because they are afraid of losing their benefit money from the government.

To my way of thinking, that's just nuts. But they can't see how much their quality of life would improve, or that God can provide for them so much more abundantly than the government would. Unfortunately some people prefer to stay stuck where they are instead of stepping out and trusting God.

Regardless of the reasons for that decision, it is still an example of mammon oriented thinking.

Biggest Difference Between Them

We should take a moment to acknowledge that the mammon system does work. You certainly can get rich in the mammon system. People do all the time.

That's why we see so many examples of mammon in our world today. Manipulation and control certainly can be used to make people rich. And many are constantly doing just that.

So please don't think I'm trying to say in this book that the Kingdom of God is the only way to get wealthily. It's not. Not by a long shot.

In fact, it's probably easier to get richer more quickly by becoming an expert in the mammon system and learning how the world's money system works than it is in the Kingdom of God.

But there is a catch, and it's huge.

That catch is perhaps the single biggest difference between the two systems. It's the baggage that comes with that wealth. The world's mammon system is cursed. Therefore wealth gained by that system comes with all kinds of baggage like selfishness, greed, isolation, disappointment, damaged relationships, regret, insignificance, despair, and the list goes on. This is why so many wealthy people who are successful by the world's standard commit suicide.

However, wealth gained by the blessing of God in His Kingdom has none of that baggage whatsoever. The Bible is clear. There is no sorrow that comes with godly wealth.

> The blessing of the Lord makes one rich,
> And He adds no sorrow with it. — Proverbs 10:22 (NKJV)

God's ways are higher than the world's ways. When it comes to financial prosperity, God's ways are far superior to the mammon system because when we line up with God's ways, He protects our hearts too. Kingdom ways protect relationships because love is the prime force, not fear like it is with mammon.

Jesus said the thief only comes to steal, kill, and destroy (John 10:10).

As we've seen, mammon is truly antichrist. That means the only way mammon will bring wealth is by stealing so much more in return. People don't realize what that mammon wealth cost them until it is far too late.

Wealth obtained from mammon destroys relationships and hardens hearts to the things of God. That's why it is especially insidious when pastors and church leaders use mammon methods to raise funds.

Manipulative offering talks and fundraising drives have no place in the Kingdom of God.

Some people see the genuine dangers of mammon and decide to reject wealth outright. But that's not the right answer either. In truth, that's a fear response. Besides, poverty theology does not line up with what the Bible clearly has to say about God and His ways.

If we're going to line our lives up with the truth of scripture, we need to find a better answer.

Fortunately, God provides ways for us to prosper and become wealthy. In Christ we can indeed prosper without succumbing to the love of money snare. I've experienced enough of it personally to know that what the Bible has to say about this is true.

More than anything else, that's what motivated me to write this book. I want to help you experience God's best and become more wealthy while avoiding mammon's traps.

Transactional vs. Relational

The mammon system is a system of buying and selling whereas the Kingdom of God is a system of giving and receiving. Mammon is transactional while the Kingdom is relational.

We could have a whole long discussion about what those particular differences look like. The one thing to keep in mind is that ministries today still must operate in a mammon run world.

This painful reality creates times when some aspects of ministry activity can effectively become transactional. In a perfect world that would not be the case. Unfortunately we operate in a fallen, imperfect world.

That means there are areas where it is effectively impossible to operate purely on a giving and receiving model and some things end up being effectively transactional, even where good ministries are concerned.

For example, the Bible college I work for intentionally keeps tuition fees low to make it accessible to as many people as possible. But we do still charge tuition. We would not be able to operate long if we didn't. And while we hate to do it, we do still dismiss students who don't pay their tuition fees.

Some organizations put on conferences and events and have faith to make them free to attend. Other organizations sell tickets. I know enough about the costs involved with hosting live events that I can see the reasons for both ways of hosting events.

You likely paid money to purchase this book. I'm here to tell you there were real costs involved in publishing it, even if you set aside all my personal time in study, life experience, teaching students, and sitting in front of a keyboard typing, etc.

Ministries have a responsibility to not only cover their operating costs and pay their staff, but to also receive provision enough to grow and positively impact more lives for the Kingdom.

If every member of the Body of Christ heard the Holy Spirit perfectly and obediently gave the exact amount He instructed at exactly the right time He said, then we could all move to a pure giving and receiving system.

Unfortunately the overwhelming majority of us do not hear and respond to God that perfectly. As a result, ministries do often find they need to charge for ministry activity and things like teaching products, etc.

That this is so often the case does not mean these ministries are ungodly or overrun with mammon. It may mean they are providing really good value, and it takes a significant amount of money for them to provide that value. And it may also mean they minister to a large number of people who don't obediently respond when God is asking those folks to give.

Unless the ministries make a habit of being manipulative in how they raise their funds, I'm willing to give them the benefit of the doubt.

Taking vs. Receiving

Because mammon is anchored in scarcity, people in the mammon system take from one another.

That's why I really do not like the phrase "take up an offering" in Christian circles. I hear it all the time, even from ministers who have a powerful revelation of the prosperity that Jesus provides for us.

I've had this conversation with many of my ministry friends. The way I see it, neither God nor Jesus take anything from anyone. Jesus Himself said it this way:

> The thief does not come except to steal, and to kill, and to destroy. I have come that they may have life, and that they may have it more abundantly. — John 10:10 (NKJV)

Taking is the something the enemy does. He's the one who steals, kills, and destroys. God only adds life. God is a giver, not a taker.

Even though God is a giver, He does indeed receive from us. For example, He receives our worship.

Jesus bore our griefs and carried our sorrows. He was wounded for our transgressions and bruised for our iniquities. It's by His stripes that we are healed.

Even so, Jesus won't take any of that from us unless we are willing to first give it to Him. Then He receives it from us.

Now I don't go around correcting pastors of churches when I hear them say, "It's time to take up the offering." I don't have jurisdiction over what they say and do in their churches. I know for a fact that God did not appoint me the offering police!

We all need to respect the limits of the authority God gives us. That means it's not our place to correct others unless we have clear authority and jurisdiction to do so.

That said, my staff at our Bible college campus know this is an area that I am passionate about. I do have both authority and jurisdiction there. We all know that if any of us say something about "taking up an offering" we wil be corrected on the spot, even if we're speaking at the front of the room when we say it.

I've warned them I will correct them if I hear it. Plus I authorized my staff to correct me on the spot if I say that myself, regardless of the circumstances. I'm human and I might slip up myself. This "take" mindset is that deeply ingrained in most of us from the worldly culture. I feel strongly enough about it that I'm willing to receive correction too if needed.

In our Bible college campus where I have authority we "receive an offering" because God only receives. He does not take from anyone.

I also tell the students about this at the beginning of the school year. In doing so, I let them know it is the role of the staff to correct one another, not their place to correct us.

As sons and daughters of God Himself, who are heirs with Christ, King Jesus our brother, we have a responsibility to create a Kingdom culture in our God-assigned area of influence and responsibility.

Receiving offerings instead of taking them is one small way we do that at our campus.

Hopefully you have ways to build a Kingdom culture in your areas of authority and jurisdiction too.

Parable of the Unjust Steward

Jesus gave us some more insight into mammon in his parable of the unjust steward in Luke chapter 16.

If you remember the story, Jesus said there was a certain rich man who found out the steward, or manager of his business was wasting his goods. The manager might have been stealing from the company for his own personal gain. Or maybe he was just not paying attention and there were significant unnecessary losses happening.

Either way, the owner decided to fire the manager.

When the manager found out, he considered his options. He knew he wasn't cut out for physical labor. But he also didn't want to experience the shame of begging for charity. So he came up with a plan.

The manager called in all the accounts that were owed to the business. But instead of requiring the account holders to pay all that they owed, he reduced each of their bills with the idea that those people would be grateful for the reduction and hopefully hire him when he was inevitably fired from his job.

Then Jesus says something rather shocking in the story.

> So the master commended the unjust steward because he had dealt shrewdly. For the sons of this world are more shrewd in their generation than the sons of light. — Luke 16:8 (NKJV)

That verse troubled me for a long time. Since the master was going to fire the guy already, why would Jesus have the master praise the guy for stealing even more from him? How is continuing to steal from the master something the master would consider wise?

When we understand the difference between the mammon system and the Kingdom of God, we can see the answers to these questions.

The master had a Kingdom mindset. He saw that money was a tool to increase the influence of the Kingdom. For the first time the manager was using money wisely. Yes, he was still stealing from the master. But this time, instead of wasting the money, he was using the money he stole as a tool to gain influence and prepare a better future for himself. For perhaps the first time in his life, the manager prioritized relationships with other people above money.

That is the best possible use of money. Jesus goes on to explain this in the next verse.

> And I say to you, make friends for yourselves by unrighteous mammon, that when you fail, they may receive you into an

everlasting home. — Luke 16:9 (NKJV)

This is the application of the parable for us. Money is simply a tool that we can use to influence our future. Even in the mammon system people understand the concept of saving for their future. We can do something even better as believers because we can literally pay it forward all the way into eternity.

We can convert temporal money in this world into changed lives, which will last for all of eternity. When we prioritize relationships with people above our money, when we use our money to bless others, that is the highest and best use of money that we can make in this life.

If that wasn't powerful enough, Jesus goes on to say something even more profound in the next few verses,

> *He who is faithful in what is least is faithful also in much; and he who is unjust in what is least is unjust also in much. Therefore if you have not been faithful in the unrighteous mammon, who will commit to your trust the true riches? And if you have not been faithful in what is another man's, who will give you what is your own?* —Luke 16:10-12 (NKJV)

Here Jesus says that money is the least thing in the Kingdom of God. People who aren't faithful in their finances will also not be faithful in the things that really matter.

So many believers want to skip past the financial issue and go straight into seeing healing, deliverance, or restored relationships. According to Jesus, it doesn't matter that people like me don't like talking about money because money is where it all starts and where we learn to how to be faithful.

According to what Jesus says here, mastering God's ways in the area of our finances will demonstrate faithfulness so that God can tust us with the true riches of His Kingdom ways in other areas too.

Perhaps it is time to do some honest reflection about our finances. Are we faithful with our finances? Or does our life move from one financial crisis to another? If the latter is the case, perhaps that is one reason why we are having trouble receiving from God in other areas of our lives too.

Jesus then closes out this teachable moment with a very powerful truth.

> "No servant can serve two masters; for either he will hate the one and love the other, or else he will be loyal to the one and despise the other. You cannot serve God and mammon." — Luke 16:13 (NKJV)

There are two systems operating simultaneously when it comes to our finances. You will serve one system or the other. According to Jesus it is impossible to serve both. You will either serve mammon or you will serve God. Choose wisely.

A Clearer Picture

One of the questions my wife Lisa has asked me over and over again in our marriage is this: "But what does that look like?"

We can talk about the theory of mammon all day long. What we really need to know is what it looks like so that we can avoid its trap.

Fortunately Paul tells us what mammon looks like when he warns Timothy about the peril that comes with the love of money.

> For the **love of money** is a root of all kinds of evil, for which some have strayed from the faith in their greediness, and pierced themselves through with many sorrows. — 1 Timothy 6:10 (NKJV)

Loving money is a root of all kinds of evil. It's not the only cause of evil. But it is definitely a big one.

Paul also told Timothy what to be wary of in these last days we are in now.

> But know this, that in the last days perilous times will come: For men will be lovers of themselves, **lovers of money,** boasters, proud, blasphemers, disobedient to parents, unthankful, unholy, unloving, unforgiving, slanderers, without self-control, brutal, despisers of good, traitors, headstrong, haughty, lovers of pleasure rather than

lovers of God, having a form of godliness but denying its power. And from such people turn away! — 2 Timothy 3:1-5 (NKJV)

Again we see the love of money in the list of ungodly traits that Paul says we are to turn away from.

We saw earlier that Jesus said we cannot serve both mammon and God. Paul gives us the key to serving God instead of serving mammon.

The key is to love God instead of loving money. According to Jesus we cannot do both. As we love one, our love for the other will necessarily dissipate.

We show our love for God in our love for one another (1 John 4:7). That means we can have one sure defense against the love of money. Always put relationships before money.

My wife and I have had numerous opportunities to put this into practice in our lives. There were several times when someone put an unjust demand on us when it came to money issues.

Back in our business days we had customers use our product or service and then when they were finished with what they needed demand their money back. It isn't always easy. And fortunately it didn't happen often. But over the years we learned to prioritize the person above the money.

That's a very valuable lesson to learn. Now we can have conversations with people about issues where money is a factor and keep a pure heart throughout the conversation and sincerely keep their best interests at heart, not the interest of our bank account.

For example, at the Bible college campus we head up we are responsible for our local budget. Student tuition is a big factor in our budget. Even so, when we are speaking with a potential student we are able to explore the best option for them to participate, and point them in the best direction regardless of whether it is attending our campus, another campus, or via an online or correspondence program. This is possible because Lisa and I learned the lesson of laying aside the love of money by prioritizing relationship with people over whatever financial benefit we might receive.

You do not have to live in fear that you will succumb to the love of money. Be vigilant. Build the habit to regularly participate in the various ways of Kingdom giving we'll be talking about in chapters four through eight. As long as you continue to put God, the people He loves, and what is in their best interest over any financial gain you might receive from a situation, you will not have to worry about becoming a lover of money.

That will hold true no matter how wealthy you become!

Chapter 2

The Power of Promises

"For all the promises of God in Him are Yes, and in Him Amen, to the glory of God through us."
— 2 Corinthians 1:20 (NKJV)

Defining Faith

In this chapter we are going to talk about the power of the promises of God and how we, as believers, can anchor our faith in those promises we see in the Bible.

I need to lay some groundwork as we start out here.

Paul said that three things will last forever: faith, hope, and love (1 Corinthians 13:13). We know that love is the greatest of the three. But for now we're going to focus on the other two.

Let's start with faith.

When we talk about something, it is important that we agree on what that term means. Faith is one of those terms that is really important for us to define. After all, faith is integral to the Christian experience. I mean we call it the Christian faith, right?

So how would you define what faith is?

That question often generates some interesting discussion. Some folks understand faith to be a purely religious term that involves sort of "checking your brain at the door of the church." They think that if you're a follower of Jesus that you must not be able to think clearly.

It's like they see faith as "disregarding all the evidence." But that's not the case, is it?

The slander of "blind faith" completely misses the mark. It's certainly not a biblical concept.

In reality, faith is exercised in all sorts of ways outside of religion. For example when an entrepreneur launches a business, they are exercising faith that their business will be profitable. Any olympic champion exercised faith that they could win the medal. No one achieves victory without some faith that it can be done by them.

However, since we are followers of Jesus, let's look at the classical biblical definition of faith found in Hebrews. Besides, it turns out it's a good starting place for any non-religious discussion of the term too.

> *Now faith is the substance of things hoped for, the evidence of things not seen.* — Hebrews 11:1 (NKJV)

From that definition we see that faith has substance. It is tangible and real.

I like how the New Living Translation presents this verse. Actually I should clarify that. I like how the copy of the New Living Translation I have on my desk presents this verse. It's an older one one published in 2004. They've since updated their translation and changed it.

Anyway, here's how they said it back then.

> *Faith is the confidence that what we hope for will actually happen; it gives us assurance about things we cannot see.* — Hebrews 11:1 (NLT, 2004 version)

There we see an aspect of faith that's not always obvious. Faith involves a level of confidence that what we believe will actually happen.

Very Similar, But Different

You see, faith is very closely related to belief. In fact, the two are so close that they often get confused with each other. Even when we look at the Bible, It can be a little less than clear, depending on the translation you happen to be reading.

For example, let's look at Matthew 17:20. If you remember the story, a man brought his boy to Jesus and says that he first took the boy to the disciples but they couldn't heal him. After Jesus cures the boy the disciples ask why they couldn't do it. Here's how the New Living Translation presents Jesus' answer,

> *"You don't have enough faith," Jesus told them. "I tell you the truth, if you had faith even as small as a mustard seed, you could say to this mountain, 'Move from here to there,' and it would move. Nothing would be impossible."* — Matthew 17:20 (NLT)

Reading that, it seems like Jesus is telling his disciples that their problem is they don't have enough faith. I mean what else can "you don't have enough faith" mean, right?

But then He goes on to explain the problem of too little faith and how to solve it by saying that we barely need any faith at all to see great miracles happen. Huh?

That doesn't make sense. Why would He acknowledge that they had any faith at all if His lesson from that "teachable moment" was that they only needed a tiny amount of faith?

How much "small as a mustard seed" faith is enough? Presented that way it makes it seem like we need some standard to measure microscopic faith in amounts even smaller than a mustard seed.

Don't know about you, but I can't make any sense of that. Now let's look at how the New King James Version translates that same verse.

> *So Jesus said to them, "Because of your unbelief; for assuredly, I say to you, if you have faith as a mustard seed, you will say to this mountain, 'Move from here to there,' and it will move; and nothing will be impossible for you.* — Matthew 17:20 (NKJV)

Here that same passage appears a whole lot less contradictory. Jesus is telling His disciples that they have a belief problem which can be countered with faith, even in small amounts.

Now that's something we can work with. All we have to do is figure out what belief and faith really are and then we can apply that lesson to our lives.

But why the difference in the translations?

It turns out there are two main sets of biblical manuscripts that translators work from to bring the English versions of scripture across from the original Greek and Hebrew languages.

These two manuscript sets are almost the same. This verse in Matthew happens to fall into that "almost" area.

The manuscripts used for translations such as the King James Version and New King James Version have the Greek word *apistia* there. That word properly translated means "unbelief" in English.

The manuscripts used for other translations such as the New Living Translation and the New International Version have the Greek word *oligopistia* there instead. That Greek word does not appear anywhere in the other set of manuscripts. It's the noun form of a word that does appear elsewhere in both sets of manuscripts as a verb, and which does mean "of little faith".

Now we could have a whole long discussion about the strengths and weaknesses of the different manuscripts and how translation works, etc. It is a worthy discussion, to be sure. But it's not one for this book.

Let's save the academic discussion for another time. I'm not here for an argument. Instead I'd rather share some practical things that help you move forward with God.

Because my point is this. It is legitimate to understand the problem as one of unbelief instead of one of too little faith. Not only is this a valid translation, but it also enables us to move towards a solution to the problem. And that's really what I believe we should be focused on, moving forward in the things of God.

I'm all about practical things that produce results in our lives.

Therefore, from my perspective, the best interpretation is that Jesus was talking about two different things: unbelief and faith.

What is Belief?

Let's take a look at those two concepts and see how they relate.

If we're going to define terms, a dictionary can be a good place to start. But in this case, even that can be challenging because the two words are so close in meaning. For example, here is how Dictonary.com defines belief

1. something believed; an opinion or conviction:

2. confidence in the truth or existence of something not immediately susceptible to rigorous proof:

3. confidence; faith; trust:

4. a religious tenet or tenets; religious creed or faith:

Personally, I think those definitions leave a little to be desired when it comes to clarity of meaning. That said, here's what I came up with for a working definition of belief,

An opinion or judgment in which a person is fully persuaded.

Our beliefs are things that we are thoroughly convinced of. Usually they are ideas and concepts that we gather as we move through life and come across information and experience.

In reality our beliefs can, and often do change over time as we gain more knowledge, and as we experience more things throughout our lives.

For example, I was a lot more sure I was right about most things when I was younger. But as I gained more life-experience I have grown to appreciate how much I truly don't know about any given subject.

Here's another way to say it. When I was sixteen I was convinced my father was wrong about a whole host of things. I confess I thought my dad was pretty idiotic about a bunch of stuff. However, as I got older, it seemed my dad got smarter and wiser about a whole host of things.

It's like my dad was a whole lot smarter guy when I was in my forties than he was back when I was a teenager.

In truth he didn't really get smarter as I got older. My dad was pretty smart the whole time. Instead it was my belief about his wisdom that changed.

There was a time in my walk with Jesus that I believed the supernatural passed away in the first century with the Apostles because that is what I was taught. That belief matched my experience at the time too.

Eventually I learned that Jesus is still in the supernatural business. As my belief in this area changed, so did my life-experiences. Now you would have a very difficult time convincing me that supernatural stuff can't happen because I've experienced too much of it first hand.

How Faith is Different

When it comes to defining faith, I again need something a little more than a dictionary definition. Here is what I came up with,

Faith is belief in action with confidence.

Or, there's another way we can explain it. I was talking about this with friends of mine who were really mathematically gifted. So I came up with this little formula:

Faith = (Belief x Action x Confidence)

Faith includes our beliefs. But it is bigger than that. If it doesn't move us to do something or say something – to actually take some kind of action – it's not really faith at all.

James said it this way,

> So you see, faith by itself isn't enough. Unless it produces good deeds, it is dead and useless. — James 2:17 (NLT)

Until we take action our "faith" is just a bunch of words. James says that unless faith produces action, it is in fact dead, or not faith at all.

As a side note, some people get confused and turned around on this point and try to do good things to generate faith. However James didn't say the good things we do produce faith. He said our faith, if it is real and alive, will naturally move us to do good things.

But I digress.

The last part of that whole faith equation is confidence. Here's what confidence means in this context,

Trust that is based on knowledge or past experience.

Basically confidence is a measure of how firmly we hold to a particular belief.

So you see how those three things come together to determine our faith at any given time. And hopefully you can now see how belief and faith are interrelated. The difference between the two is subtle. But understanding it brings a whole lot more clarity to things that Jesus said, such as Matthew 17:20 above.

When we believe the truth with enough confidence to take action we exercise faith. And it doesn't take much of that faith to see huge things happen, even miraculous things.

Now hopefully you can see where unbelief, that is believing things that aren't true – believing lies – completely clogs up the working of our faith. Unbelief prevents us from ever seeing the miraculous in our lives.

Too often we spend time and energy trying to increase our faith when Jesus said that's not really our problem. We pray and plead with God, begging Him to give us more faith.

But our problem is really with unbelief, not a lack of faith.

Faith vs. Belief

Belief is *what* we hold on to. For the most part, our beliefs are evidence based. Some people even go so far as to say, "seeing is believing."

Faith, on the other hand, kicks in when we get to the end of the evidence. It is the *how* behind the things we believe before we have concrete evidence for them.

Take skydiving for example. We may believe that a parachute will get us to the ground safely when we jump out of an airplane. That belief might be based on talking with folks who have done it. Maybe we've studied aerodynamics to know the theory behind how parachutes work. We might have even jumped out of planes before and experienced floating safely to the ground with a parachute.

However, the moment we jump out of the plane we have faith that our parachute will open when we pull the ripcord. It hasn't happened yet, but we sure hope it will!

Faith is what connects the evidence to our beliefs when the evidence doesn't quite get us all the way there, like in that moment when we're free falling before the parachute canopy has deployed above us.

The opposite of belief is unbelief. You might dispute facts like skydiving being statistically safer than driving a car. Perhaps you look at the evidence and decide that it's nuts to jump out of a perfectly good airplane. Then you wouldn't believe that skydiving is for you.

However, the opposite of faith is not *un*faith. The opposite of faith is *fear*.

Maybe you look at all the evidence and truly believe that skydiving is safe. You know that parachutes get people to the ground without incident every day and that it is more dangerous to drive your car. But in spite of all the facts, all the evidence, there is no way you are ever going to jump out of an airplane because the thought of free falling thousands of feet above the ground terrifies you.

You can believe all the right things about skydiving but never actually do it because you lack faith. If you had faith, it would overcome your fear.

Where it gets interesting and weird is the reality that faith can even cause us to believe things in spite of the evidence.

This causes problems for some because sometimes people believe goofy things that are simply untrue.

However we all know stories about people who believed and persevered in the face of overwhelming odds when everyone around them thought they were nuts. Yet in the end, they were shown to be right.

We tend to say that people like that have great faith.

On a small scale, all the evidence seems to be saying that you are going to die when you jump out of that airplane. However you jump anyway because you have faith that the parachute will open in time to save you.

Wired for Faith

Human beings are hard wired for faith. We all have core sets of beliefs. Some are based on more evidence than others.

And sometimes new evidence may come to light. When that happens, some folks change their beliefs.

Others exercise faith and cling to their beliefs despite the new evidence.

Pick any controversial topic and you'll find passionate people on both sides of the debate who have followed the evidence as far as it will go and then have faith to get the rest of the way to their conclusions.

To me it seems that faith is inescapable. We all have faith in something.

Even atheists have beliefs. They are certain that God does not exist. Honestly, someone who believes that the amazing creation around us, which has both intricate complexity and incredible precision at the same time, all came about because of random chance has far more faith than I can muster up.

When you think about it, basic observation shows us that complex things that are truly random are also always very chaotic. Yet we see incredible precision all around us in creation.

For example, all the uncountable stars and other astronomical bodies in the universe move with such precision that their movements can be accurately determined with mathematical formulas. The Bible says God gave that precision to the moon and stars. The human eye has hundreds of millions of cells with many different specialized types. Yet the shape of the eyeball is precisely configured within very tight tolerances to provide clear focused vision.

The atheist who chooses to believe all that precise complexity came about through random chance has far more faith to believe despite the evidence than I do.

If we are going to believe without solid proof, then the key is to make sure what you believe is indeed true. When your faith is rooted in unshakable truth then you can live without fear and be so peaceful that it might not even make sense to folks around you. Jesus said it this way,

> *And you shall know the truth, and the truth shall make you free.* —
> John 8:32 (NKJV)

The more certainty we can add to the equation that what we believe is, in fact, the truth, the more confidence we can have in our beliefs. That creates an incredibly powerful combination.

Think about it. Having those two nailed down — believing something that's true, and therefore having strong confidence in our belief — covers two thirds of the faith equation. At that point we don't need much action at all to produce some really big faith!

Fortunately for us as believers and followers of Jesus we have a source that we can be certain is true!

I think you can see where we are going with this. But before we get there, I want to add one more piece to the puzzle. Do you remember what we said faith is back at the beginning of this chapter?

> *Now faith is the substance of things hoped for, the evidence of things not seen.* — Hebrews 11:1 (NKJV)

Substance of Things Hoped For

Let's talk for a moment about hope because I think hope gets a bad rap in most Christian circles, especially in the charismatic world. Have you ever seen someone get reprimanded for saying, "I hope so!" by someone else who told them they need to have faith, not hope?

Please. Don't do that.

Remember 1 Corinthians 13:13 where we started this chapter? Hope is one of the three things that will last forever, along with faith and love. Since hope is eternal, then we shouldn't be hassling folks who cling to it.

One of the big reasons so many believers don't value hope as they should is that the world has a very different understanding of what hope is from the biblical meaning. In the world we might say, "I hope I win the lottery," or "I hope I don't get a speeding ticket."

Really what we're saying is, *"I wish I would win the lottery… But I know the odds are so far against it that I don't really think I will."* We see hope as a feeling or a desire that something might work out… but we know probably won't.

The biblical meaning of the word is different. In the New Testament, the Greek word that is translated "hope" is *elpis*. That word carries with it an expectation that the desired outcome will actually come to pass.

This is far more powerful than a simple wish or desire.

When the Bible talks about hope it is referring to something that is anticipated with pleasure.

As believers we anticipate how wonderful heaven is going to be. Because of what we see in the Bible we expect that God will reward us because we earnestly seek him.

When we see promises in the Bible we can get excited and truly expect them to come to pass. We read the words of Jesus and the apostles in the New Testament and we linger over them, knowing they are true, anticipating how they are impacting our lives.

There are times when life's storms rage around us. Like a mariner in a stormy sea at night catching a first glimpse of a lighthouse for a bearing, we can plot a true course based on God's word. We can expect a good end even when it looks like all is lost because we know from the Bible that God is for us.

This is what true biblical hope is all about.

Hope Related to Faith

Like belief, hope is also related to faith as we see in Hebrews 11:1. Faith is real, tangible. It has "substance."

Hope is the precursor to faith. It leads the way, and opens the door to faith. In fact, I don't think it's too big a stretch to say faith wouldn't exist without it, which may very well be why Paul included hope in the list of eternal stuff.

Let me paint a word picture here that might help you see how these two things are related. My background is in the maritime industry. I worked in and around ocean going cargo ships for a couple decades.

One of the things I saw every day was ships tying up to the dock. It's amazing to see a huge ship displacing tens of thousands of tons held to the dock with just a handful of mooring lines, which are basically just big ropes.

Those massive ships that carry cargo all around the world are held tight against the pier with as few as six lines.

Our faith is like those mooring lines, solid. Our faith connects the spiritual solidly into the natural. It pulls those spiritual truths into the physical world so they become reality in our own lives.

The thing is those mooring lines are heavy. They are too big for one man to move around a ship's deck by himself. It takes a team of guys and some very powerful winches to move those lines around the decks of the ships.

Then there's the problem of getting those heavy lines across to the dock where they can be attached to the bollards to hold the ship in place. It's not like you can just throw a six inch diameter rope.

So what they do is tie a smaller rope to the mooring line and throw that across. The smaller line is about the diameter of a clothes line and is called a "heaving line". It has a special knot at the end called a monkey's fist. The monkey's fist gives it some weight and makes it much easier to throw longer distances.

Then the guys on the dock pull on the heaving line to get to the heavier mooring line, which they in turn place over a bollard on the dock.

Hope is like those heaving lines. It connects us to our faith, bridges the gap between the faith that brings spiritual realities into being and our limited belief in the natural.

Heaving lines won't hold the ship to the dock. They're far too small. That's not even their function.

In the same way hope won't make spiritual truths manifest in the physical. But that's OK because that's what faith does.

Hope is still vitally important, though, because we need it in order to realize our faith. Remember Hebrews 11:1 above? Hope is pre-faith.

One day I was talking about this with my wife Lisa. She was a veterinary technician, or veterinary nurse, for a number of years, so she tends to frame things in animal terms. She said hope is like faith in the larval state 'cause it's not fully developed yet. (I'm not sure if that analogy works or not.)

But I do find it interesting that the Old Testament Hebrew word for hope is *ṭiqwâ*. Turns out that hope is the translation of that word in the figurative sense.

The literal meaning of that Hebrew word is "a cord."

It's almost like God had the picture of a ship and heaving lines in mind when he created hope in the very beginning.

The True Power of Hope

Why is hope so powerful and enduring? Because it is anchored in the very presence of God, His word, and His promises. Look at what this passage has to say about hope,

> *This hope we have as an anchor of the soul, both sure and steadfast, and which enters the Presence behind the veil, where the forerunner has entered for us, even Jesus, having become High Priest forever according to the order of Melchizedek.* — Hebrews 6:19-20 (NKJV)

Hope will endure because God endures. Our hope reaches all the way up into heaven, and into the Holy of Holies where it is connected to (and connects us to) His very presence in Heaven. Therefore hope connects us to God Himself.

True biblical hope, with its joyful anticipation, is an incredibly powerful tool for our walk with God. It bridges the gap when our faith isn't all it could be and keeps us connected to Him.

There may be an area in your life where your faith isn't fully developed yet, where you haven't seen the manifestation of the thing you long for in your life. I want to encourage you, take hope. Hold on to hope.

Even if you are all the way down at the end of the line, cling to that monkey's fist and don't let go. That hope is connected to the very throne room of God Himself. Your ship *will* come in. Your faith will grow. That thing will become manifest if only you refuse to despair of hope.

As we've seen, the key to being successful in all this is finding the truth. When our mooring lines of faith are made fast to the ship of truth, we can tighten them up, pull that ship secure against the dock, and see things transfer from the spiritual into the natural.

The good news is that, as followers of Jesus, we have a source of truth that we can lock into with confidence. We have God's word.

Here are a few of the many Bible verses that attest to the truth of God's word,

> Your righteousness is an everlasting righteousness, and Your law is truth. — Psalms 119:142 (NKJV)

> You are near, O Lord, and all Your commandments are truth. — Psalms 119:151 (NKJV)

> The entirety of Your word is truth, and every one of Your righteous judgments endures forever. — Psalms 119:160 (NKJV)

> And now, O Lord God, You are God, and Your words are true, and You have promised this goodness to Your servant. — 2 Samuel 7:28 (NKJV)

> Sanctify them by Your truth. Your word is truth. — John 17:17 (NKJV)

Therefore we know God's word is true.

But more than that, it's in God's word that we find truth. When it comes to seeing our prayers answered, when it comes to seeing our faith manifest as we pull things from the supernatural, spiritual world into the natural, physical world we want to pay special attention to the promises of God.

Promises

When we talk about the promises of God, this is perhaps the most critical truth we need to keep at the forefront of our minds:

> For all the promises of God in Him are Yes, and in Him Amen, to the glory of God through us. — 2 Corinthians 1:20 (NKJV)

All the promises of God are yes and amen **in Jesus**, not in us. The promises are already guaranteed on our behalf because of the finished work of Jesus on the cross. This includes the Old Testament promises too!

That means we can read through the Bible, and when we see a promise on its pages, we can take it to the bank.

Do you understand how powerful that is?

Because Jesus was who He was, and did what He did, we now have access to every promise and blessing He deserved when we appropriate them by faith.

Wait. Some of you still aren't sure. OK, then. Turn in your Bible to Galatians 3. Look here at verse 13,

> *Christ has redeemed us from the curse of the law, having become a curse for us (for it is written, "Cursed is everyone who hangs on a tree"), that the blessing of Abraham might come upon the Gentiles in Christ Jesus, that we might receive the promise of the Spirit through faith.* — Galatians 3:13-14 (NKJV)

When Jesus went to the cross He rescued us from all of the curses that come from the old system of the Law. He took all the curses we deserve on our behalf.

Then what does it say there in verse 14? He did all that so all the blessing of Abraham would come on us, and so that we might receive the what? The promise. (There's that word again!)

How do we receive that promise? Through faith!

For example, look at all the promises in Deuteronomy chapter 28. That chapter basically records the terms of the Old Covenant that the Israelites agreed to with Moses and God. The chapter is a list of blessings and curses. Those who kept the covenant by obeying all the laws get the blessings. And those who broke the law set themselves up to receive the curses.

Every one of the first 14 verses of Deuteronomy chapter 28 are highlighted in my electronic Bibles. Every time I go to that chapter I see a rainbow of happy colors leaping off the screen at me.

And that's appropriate because those first 14 verses list the blessings. The good news is that you and I don't have to keep the law to receive those promises and their blessings.

As believers we are now in Christ. Since Jesus obeyed the law perfectly, and we're in Christ, it's as if we did obey the law perfectly too. As we saw in that passage from Galatians just above, Jesus became the curse that we deserved, so that now we can be blessed instead. Jesus did the work of obedience, and we get the blessings obedience brings!

Now that's good news indeed!

Inheriting the Kingdom of God

The promises of God are vital for us to inherit the Kingdom of God.

Some Christians get tripped up with this concept of inheriting the Kingdom. There are a couple different places in the Bible where Paul lists some fleshly, sinful behavior and then says that people who do those things won't inherit the Kingdom of God. (See 1 Corinthians 6:9-10 and Galatians 5:19-21.)

Some folks interpret that to mean that we can lose our salvation. No! That's not what those passages mean.

There is a difference between entering a house and inheriting it, right? You can live in the house your entire life without ever actually inheriting it.

In the same way you can be saved, and enter into the Kingdom of God, but not *inherit* the Kingdom.

Yet which is more valuable — living in the house, or inheriting it? I think it's pretty obvious that inheriting a house is far better than simply having the use of it to live in. Inheriting the house means you've inherited the wealth.

Here's another way to say it. Living in the house means you are still going to heaven when you die. Inheriting the house means you also get to enjoy the fullness of everything Jesus has made available to you in this life.

In theological terms, we're talking about the difference between salvation and sanctification. Salvation gets you in the door. But inheriting the Kingdom involves the process of sanctification.

Do you want to know how to inherit the Kingdom of God? Peter tells us the answer to that question,

> *Grace and peace be multiplied to you in the knowledge of God and of Jesus our Lord, as His divine power has given to us all things that pertain to life and godliness, through the knowledge of Him who called us by glory and virtue, by which have been given to us exceedingly great and precious promises,* **that through these** *you may be partakers of the divine nature, having escaped the corruption that is in the world through lust.* — 2 Peter 1:2-4 (NKJV)

Everything we need for life and godliness comes from the knowledge of God and how His Kingdom operates. The more we come to understand the Kingdom of God and align our lives, thoughts, and actions with the Kingdom, the more of the Kingdom resources will come our way. I'm talking about *all* the resources of the Kingdom — wealth, health, wisdom, favor, good relationships — you name it.

And it all works on the principle of promises. That's how we get to the abundant life.

To the degree that you have knowledge of God and how His Kingdom operates is the degree that your prayers will be answered. We'll talk more about God answering our prayers in the next chapter.

Inheriting the Promises

Wait. That passage told us how to be partakers of the divine nature (through the promises). But how to we *inherit* those promises?

I'm glad you asked. Take a look at this passage in the book of Hebrews.

*And we desire that each one of you show the same diligence to the full assurance of hope until the end, that you do not become sluggish, but imitate those **who through faith and patience inherit the promises.** — Hebrews 6:11-12 (NKJV)*

That last phrase tells us the answer we are looking for. We inherit the promises, meaning we take possession of them and see them manifest in our lives, through faith and patience.

We've already seen earlier in this chapter what faith is and how it works. In addition, we know that patience is a fruit of the Spirit (Galatians 5:22). So that's already inside us, waiting to be let out.

We receive the promises of God by faith, just like Abraham. We see them in the Word of God. We speak them out. We chose to believe them. We apply the confidence of knowing that promise has already been answered Yes and Amen by God Himself because we are in Christ.

Then it's time to get into action. We must do something in the natural to take a step towards that promise.

It is at that moment when we step out that our faith starts to kick in.

What we do next is critical. This is the point where so many believers miss their promise. According to Hebrews 6:12, the thing to do is to persevere. We hold fast to that promise until.

Until what? Until we see it move from the spiritual into the natural in our lives.

And let us not grow weary while doing good, for in due season we shall reap if we do not lose heart. — Galatians 6:9 (NKJV)

Lose heart means to become discouraged, to lose hope or confidence.

The promises of God are powerful. They are a solid vessel of truth that we can tie our faith into as we bring those promises out of the spiritual realm and into the natural realm.

You may be wondering what any of this has to do with finances or money. I assure you that getting your mind around what we covered in this chapter will help you see some amazing practical results when we combine it with what we'll cover in the rest of the book.

This foundation is worth laying. Because when we start to build up and go vertical, we'll get to build far higher than we would otherwise.

Two Kinds of Promises

It's important to point out that the promises of God can be sorted into two general categories. Some promises of God are unconditional.

With unconditional promises, there is nothing we need to do on our end for those promises to apply to our lives, assuming we are already born again. For example, Jesus says that He is with us always, even to the end of the age (Matthew 28:20). In addition, God says "I will never leave you or forsake you." (Hebrews 13:5)

These promises are unconditional. There is nothing we need to do to inherit these promises and experience them in our lives, assuming we are already believers. We simply believe these unconditional promises and receive them.

But other promises of God have one or more conditions attached. For example, the Bible says, *"If you confess with your mouth that Jesus is Lord and believe in your heart that God raised him from the dead, you will be saved."* (Romans 10:9)

Not everyone is automatically saved. The word "if" at the beginning means there are a couple conditions attached to that promise:

1.   One must confess with their mouth that Jesus is Lord.

2.   One must also believe in their heart that God raised Jesus from the dead.

Once those two conditions are met, then we can receive the promise, *"you will be saved."*

That means we must use our brains when we see a promise in the Bible to determine which category it belongs to. Any promise that is unconditional, we can just receive. For other promises that have conditions, we need to look at those conditions and see if we meet the conditions to qualify. If not, we may need to do something, or change something so that we qualify.

Sometimes it may look at first glance like we don't meet the condition(s) of a promise. But when we look deeper into scripture we find that we do actually meet the conditions.

Deuteronomy 28 is a great example. The promises in the first 14 verses are contingent on obeying the Law. So it might seem that we don't qualify. I don't know about you, but I don't do all the stuff laid out in the Old Covenant.

For example:

> And all these blessings shall come upon you and overtake you, because you obey the voice of the Lord your God — Deuteronomy 28:2 (NKJV)

However, Jesus fulfilled the Law perfectly on our behalf because we are now "in Christ." That means that we are indeed entitled to receive all of those promises because it's as though we kept the law.

Now that we are in Christ we can read that passage as if it said this,

> And all these blessings shall come upon you and overtake you, because [Jesus obeyed] the voice of the Lord your God

It means that when we see conditional promises where Jesus has met the condition on our behalf, we can just receive them as if they were unconditional promises. That is an amazing truth right there!

Here's an example of a conditional promise were we must do something to meet the condition.

> He who has pity on the poor lends to the Lord, and He will pay back what he has given. — Proverbs 19:17 (NKJV)

God promises to pay back what we give to the poor. However, until we actually give to the poor in the first place, we have not yet met the condition required for God to pay us back.

Jesus does not meet that condition for us. It's up to us. No amount of faith can receive that promise until the conditions are met.

So as you can see, it is important for us to engage our brains when we find God's promises in the Bible. We must determine whether the promise is conditional or unconditional.

If there are conditions tied to the promise we must look at whether or not we already meet that condition (for example when Jesus met the condition already on our behalf). If we do not meet the condition, then we can look at what adjustments we must make in our lives so that we meet the condition God put on that particular promise before we can receive it.

Make Room for Faith to Grow

There are a couple more things about faith that we should talk about before we move on to the next chapter. We see them in this parable about the Kingdom that Jesus shared,

> Jesus also said, "The Kingdom of God is like a farmer who scatters seed on the ground. Night and day, while he's asleep or awake, the seed sprouts and grows, but he does not understand how it happens. The earth produces the crops on its own. First a leaf blade pushes through, then the heads of wheat are formed, and finally the grain ripens. And as soon as the grain is ready, the farmer comes and harvests it with a sickle, for the harvest time has come." — Mark 4:26-29 (NLT)

First, when we get into the promises of God as they relate to finances, it's OK if we are like the farmer Jesus described here. We don't need to know exactly how God does what He does before we can believe it works and see results. The farmer may not understand exactly how his crops germinate and grow. But that does not prevent him from receiving his harvest when it does.

In the same way, I can't explain exactly how God gets His promises to us when we believe them. But that doesn't keep me from receiving those promises by faith. A while back I made the decision not to let the things I don't understand prevent me from receiving what I do understand.

The other thing we see in this parable is the production of a harvest is a process. The farmer doesn't see fully formed grain pushing out of the ground. Instead the plants first sprout and break through the surface of the soil. They continue to grow and mature over time until they can support the grain. The grain does not ripen until after it is formed. We must allow for that process and make room for our faith to grow.

Part of the process is allowing time for it to happen.

It's true that we receive that promise in the spiritual realm the moment we pray and release our faith for it. Jesus said it this way,

> *Therefore I say to you, whatever things you ask when you pray, believe that you receive them, and you will have them.* — Mark 11:24 (NKJV)

There He says we are to believe we receive them, "when we pray." So the moment we pray the prayer of faith we receive the thing in the spiritual realm.

Even so, it is not unusual for some amount of time that passes between the time we release our faith for something and we see it in our lives in the natural. This is the gap between, "amen" and, "there it is!"

During that time, it is critical that we remain in a position of faith. It is our faith that pulls that thing across from the spiritual into the natural world. Do not let yourself get discouraged or deceived by the enemy that it didn't really happen. Trust the mooring lines of your faith to pull that ship of promise tight to the dock.

The other part of the process involves honesty with yourself and with God about what you really believe. Our faith grows over time just like the crop in that parable of Jesus grows over time.

This means that we learn to believe God for big things by first believing Him for smaller things. For example, it will be very difficult for you to successfully believe God to provide $2 million profit to you through a business until you've experienced running a business first.

David exercised his faith when he killed the lion and the bear before he faced Goliath.

Make it a point to believe God for some small things. Then you will have more confidence in God's promises as you believe for bigger things. Writing down those victories can also help strengthen your faith too because you can go back and review the victories God gave you in the past as you are moving into a position of faith for something bigger.

Writing things down also helps you remember your own stories when you want to share them with others to encourage them in their own faith walk as they step into receiving God's promises. It helps make your journey with God come alive!

Chapter 3

God Glorified in Answering Prayers

"And whatever you ask in My name, that I will do, that the Father may be glorified in the Son."
— John 14:13 (NKJV)

About That Gospel

In this chapter we are going to address a misconception in the Body of Christ that asking for specific things in prayer is selfish. It turns out that is simply not true. We're going to look at why that's the case.

Towards the beginning of the book we talked about the Gospel. Do you remember what the Gospel is?

The Gospel is the Kingdom of God. It's good news when we tell people about the Kingdom of God, how it works, and more importantly, how they can participate in the Kingdom. The Kingdom of God is really the only message Jesus preached.

Remember, salvation is just the doorway into the Kingdom. I mean you can't get into the Kingdom of God without entering it, so salvation, what Jesus called being born again, is vital. And it's certainly not bad news that we have the opportunity to spend eternity in the presence of God instead of in eternal torment.

While it is indeed good news, going to Heaven instead of Hell when we die is not really the Gospel, because there's so much more to it than that. We have an entire Kingdom to explore!

Let's try to use our imaginations here for a moment and pretend that you are Jesus. I mean I know that each one of us is like Jesus. 1 John 4:17 tells us that. And we have the mind of Christ too (1 Corinthians 2:16).

But let's just pretend for a moment that you actually *are* Jesus. You've already been through the cross and conquered sin and death. You've already been resurrected too.

You know you've got a short time with your followers before you hand off to the Holy Spirit and head back to Heaven. What are you going to talk with them about?

What's the most important thing you want them to understand so that they can be best equipped to fulfill the mission you've assigned them?

Fortunately, we don't have to guess. Luke wrote it down for us.

> *The former account I made, O Theophilus, of all that Jesus began both to do and teach, until the day in which He was taken up, after He through the Holy Spirit had given commandments to the apostles whom He had chosen, to whom He also presented Himself alive after His suffering by many infallible proofs, being seen by them during forty days and speaking of the things pertaining to* **the kingdom of God**. — Acts 1:1-3 (NKJV)

Right there we see that the big thing on the mind of Jesus, the primary topic He wanted to drive home to the disciples was the Kingdom of God. If the Kingdom of God was so important to Jesus right before He ascended to Heaven, do you think it might be worth learning about today? I think so.

Father's Good Pleasure

It turns out, Jesus isn't the only one interested in the Kingdom of God. The Father is very interested in His Kingdom too. In fact, the Father cares so much about His Kingdom that He entrusts it to the most capable hands He can find here on planet Earth — you and me.

Look at these words of Jesus,

> Do not fear, little flock, for it is your Father's good pleasure to give you the kingdom. — Luke 12:32 (NKJV)

"Do not fear." Faith drives out fear. Knowing the promises deep down gives us faith. God wants us to receive the Kingdom. It gives Him pleasure to see us operate in Kingdom ways. This glorifies God because when we do things that give God pleasure it glorifies Him.

When we prosper in the Kingdom it pleases and glorifies God.

> Let them shout for joy and be glad,
> Who favor my righteous cause;
> And let them say continually,
> "Let the Lord be magnified,
> Who has pleasure in the prosperity of His servant." — Psalms 35:27 (NKJV)

God takes pleasure in our prosperity.

The word translated "prosperity" in this verse means more than just finances. It is the Hebrew word *shalom*. It means safe, well, happy, friendly, health, prosperity, and peace. It's the whole shooting match.

God takes pleasure when we experience all of that.

Next, look at these words from the prophet Haggai.

> Go up to the mountains and bring wood and build the temple, that I may take pleasure in it and be glorified," says the Lord. — Haggai 1:8 (NKJV)

There we see that when we give God pleasure, it also glorifies Him.

What did we see earlier in Luke 12:32 is the Father's good pleasure? Giving us the Kingdom.

Therefore, when we receive and inherit the Kingdom of God, we are really glorifying God because we are pleasing Him.

I took the time to explain this because some people have a twisted belief that it is somehow selfish to receive stuff from God. Or they might think it's OK to receive intangible spiritual things, but just not material stuff or something like healing of a malady that would improve their quality of life.

If you've thought that way in the past, think about this. Is it ever selfish to bring glory to God?

It's not. And since bringing glory to God is never a selfish thing, and since it brings glory to God when you receive the Kingdom through His promises, then it is not selfish of you to desire the absolute best the Kingdom has to offer you. The more of the Kingdom of God you receive, the more pleasure and glory you bring to your Father in Heaven!

Fruit of Answered Prayers

Have you ever thought about what brings glory to God? Jesus says there is something else that also brings glory to the Father too. Take a look at this verse from the gospel of John,

> By this My Father is glorified, that you bear much fruit; so you will be My disciples. — John 15:8 (NKJV)

Our Father is glorified when we "bear much fruit." That begs the question, what fruit do we bear?

Typically when I ask this question in class, the Bible college students will answer that our fruit is the souls we bring with us by introducing them to Jesus. And it is true that we absolutely are called to make disciples and a huge part of that discipleship process is bringing people to the Lord.

Others will point to the fruit of love, joy peace, patience, kindness, goodness, gentleness, and self-control. That's the fruit of the Spirit, and yes, we definitely should be bearing that fruit in our lives too.

However, Jesus is talking here about us bearing very specific fruit that is different from all that. We know this because He tells us exactly what He means just a few verses later in that same chapter.

> *You did not choose Me, but I chose you and appointed you that you should go and bear fruit, and that your fruit should remain, that whatever you ask the Father in My name He may give you.* — John 15:16 (NKJV)

The fruit that we are to bear in abundance specifically because it brings glory to God is the fruit of answered prayers, that whatever you ask the Father in Jesus' name, He may give you. We are called to bear the fruit of answered prayers because when our prayers are answered it glorifies God.

And just in case you don't want to hang your hat on just one verse, Jesus also says the same thing in an earlier chapter.

> *And whatever you ask in My name, that I will do, that the Father may be glorified in the Son.* — John 14:13 (NKJV)

Our Father is eager to answer your prayers because doing so brings Him glory. That's over and above His loving desire to bless you.

Power of Specific Prayers

Let me point out that the more specific we can get in our prayers, the more God will be glorified when He answers them.

Think about it. When we pray vague, general prayers, "God, please bless me with good stuff," how do we know God is coming through on those? I mean we can *believe* it's God, and we can *say* it's God. But how do we *know*?

Honestly, that's a bit of a challenge amongst Christians today. Our prayers are so vague and general that there isn't much of a testimony when God answers them.

For example, I can't tell you how many times I've heard folks pray for "traveling mercies" when someone was heading out on a trip. That's really vague. What does it look like when God answers that prayer?

What kind of testimony is produced? "My flights were all on time. Praise God!"

Yes, praise God indeed. But honestly, that's not a very compelling testimony to someone who doesn't know God. Flights are supposed to be on time.

When we start getting specific with our prayers and adding details, and then things end up happening just like we prayed down to those details, then it is much harder for someone to say it was "coincidence" that we prayed and then those things happened in just that way.

Take the traveling example. There are all kinds of specific things we can ask God for where our trip is concerned. Maybe we want to have a restful flight so we arrive at our destination fully charged and ready to jump into whatever assignment God has for us there.

Or maybe we could ask for God to give us opportunities to encourage others we encounter during our trip who might be stressed from traveling. Or you can ask that He seats you next to someone for you to minister to. Or maybe someone who is quiet so you can rest.

Really, there is an endless variety of things we can pray to add more specificity. The more we practice this, the more effective our prayers become.

The key here is praying with boldness. As we saw in the last chapter, one of the best ways to ensure we have confidence in what we believe is to base our beliefs in God's word. Praying God's word back to Him is an incredibly powerful way to see your prayers answered.

For far too long the Body of Christ has held back from praying bold, faith-filled prayers because of a false sense of humility. Reject that ungodly lie that says bold prayers are selfish. Pray boldly and very specifically. Then watch God show up and answer those prayers.

Then tell everyone what an awesome God you serve. Share how He answers your prayers down to the last detail, and watch how much He is glorified in the process.

Our prayers can, and should, make a difference in our lives and in the lives of those around us. The great Scottish protestant reformer, John Knox was known as a powerful man of prayer. So much so, that he struck fear in the hearts of monarchs in his day.

One of those who feared the prayers of John Knox was Mary, Queen of Scots. She reportedly said, "I fear John Knox's prayers more than all the assembled armies of Europe."

Like Knox, you too can change your world by praying bold and specific prayers.

Remember, it brings God glory to answer your prayers. He's not intimidated by you getting specific. In fact, the more specific you get in your prayers, the more obvious it becomes to everyone around you that God is the one answering. When you get very specific with your prayers, you very effectively remove the possibility that random chance can account for the results you see.

Let me add just one last thought before I share some examples from my own life.

Our faith is built over time from victory to victory. If you've never been very specific with God in your prayers before, it may take a while before you see bang-on perfect results. If some of the details aren't there the very first time, remember that you are far closer than you would have been with your old generic prayers.

Keep your attention focused on the victories you do win, rather than looking at the perfection you might fall a bit short of. This way your faith will grow and you will find yourself with the faith to believe God for some amazingly specific things in a relatively short amount of time.

Your Words Have Power Too

The true power of faith filled words is something that I did not fully understand or appreciate for a long time. I grew up as an only child, I'm a natural introvert, and I tend to process information internally by thinking things through rather than talking them out.

I had the idea that God knows my thoughts anyway, so I didn't see the value in saying things out loud.

However, there is genuine power is speaking words aloud in faith. An entire book and then some could be written on just this topic alone.

> *For assuredly, I say to you, whoever says to this mountain, 'Be removed and be cast into the sea,' and does not doubt in his heart, but believes that those things he says will be done, he will have whatever he says.* — Mark 11:23 (NKJV)

While it is absolutely vital that we have belief in our heart for the things we pray for, at the same time, Jesus tells us a couple of things in that verse. Frist He tells us to speak to the mountain, not merely think about it. Then he goes on to say we will have whatever we *say*, not whatever we think. I've seen that in scripture for a long time. I've also heard many teachings about the power of our words. And yet I still had a tendency not to speak out my own prayers.

Not speaking out my prayers negatively affected the results I experienced. I understand that now.

When we go all the way back to the beginning in Genesis chapter one we see that God created the entire universe by speaking it into existence. Over and over again we see the phrase, "then God said..." in the first chapter.

God created us in His image. Our words are powerful too. Proverbs says it this way,

> *Death and life are in the power of the tongue,*
> *And those who love it will eat its fruit.* — Proverbs 18:21 (NKJV)

Your words literally have the power to add life, or add death to people and situations. Because you are a follower of Jesus and have been adopted into God's own family, your words are empowered with great authority.

Therefore, as we go through these sections and you see the various ways you can release your faith in these promises of God that are presented in the remainder of the book, remember to speak your faith out verbally.

When you speak out your faith in God's promises, and your words match what you believe in your own heart, you will see amazing things happen.

I've learned the importance of this the hard way. A big part of the cause of my inconsistent early results happened when I did not declare my faith out loud when I gave, even though I was giving in the different ways described later in this book.

Now, I make it a point to speak a faith declaration over my giving. Sometimes it's just a whispered prayer. We don't have to shout to exercise our authority.

But now that I do declare my faith I see much more consistent results, praise God!

Examples of Three Houses

Lisa and I learned the value of praying specifically through trial and error. God helped us see this through the last three houses we have lived in. I'll share these stories here to hopefully encourage you too.

We start with what we call the smelly house.

By the time Lisa and I finished Bible college, we knew that God was calling us to Scotland to open a campus of the Bible college there. The school we graduated from had moved about a forty minute drive up into the mountains outside of Colorado Springs during our third year.

Lisa had been hired on to help with the events team at the school. That meant long days when conferences were on. Plus we knew we would need to be on campus a fair amount for meetings and whatnot too.

We prayed about it and felt we should move up the mountain closer to the school. Woodland Park is a relatively small town. When the school moved, there weren't a lot of places to rent.

From our perspective the challenge was that we had a pet cat at the time. Most of the rentals we saw wouldn't allow cats.

So we prayed what we later realized was a very vague prayer, asking God for a two bedroom place in Woodland Park that would allow our cat. I worked from home at the time, so we needed the extra bedroom for an office.

It took a few months of looking. But we finally found a place that was being renovated. The location wasn't ideal. But we figured we would be moving to Scotland at some point. So it wasn't really a permanent move.

On the Saturday we moved in, there was a chemically smell to the place. We just assumed it was because they painted and put down a nice new floor. It was summer in Colorado. So we just left the windows open and figured it would air out in a couple days.

Only it didn't. The smell really bothered Lisa. So she got busy unpacking and hanging pictures on the walls, and whatnot.

I thought Lisa was overreacting, and that caused some friction between us. On the Thursday I needed to record some audio for a project with my work. Lisa was on the phone, so I closed my office door. There was also some street noise, so I closed the window too.

Within twenty minutes I was loopy from the fumes. I came out of the office and my face was all red too.

I had to admit Lisa was right. It was serious. Something wasn't right with that place.

Our landlord came over the next day and was stunned. He had no idea the problem was there. But he did the right thing and said that he wouldn't hold us to the lease we signed because it was dangerous to our health.

The problem was that it took us months to find that place. What were we going to do?

Looking back, we received what we prayed for. Unfortunately we had very low expectations and therefore saw very poor results.

Talking to some friends about our dilema, they suggested we get specific. So I opened up a shared document and Lisa and I typed up a list of what we wanted in a new place. We weren't extravagant. But we were specific.

For example, I wanted a shower head that I could stand under without having to bend down like I did for the three years in our previous apartment. We wanted quiet neighbors.

One of Lisa's important items was that the new place would have the peace of God when we saw it. Our list ended up with twenty eight items. When we were finished, we prayed and asked God to show us the new place that matched our list.

That was on Friday evening.

The next morning Lisa chatted with a girlfriend of hers and shared our housing challenge. Turns out that her friend's parents owned a place and their tenants were moving out that very day.

Long story short, the new place had twenty four and a half things on our list. Lisa found a pad of paper in one of the kitchen drawers and the previous tenant left a note that said, "Welcome! This is God's place of peace!"

We moved in the next day and lived in that place of peace for the two and a half years it took for us to transition overseas to the mission field.

So here's what we saw. When we prayed a very general prayer it took us months of looking to find the smelly house. Once we got specific, we found a place that had twenty four and a half out of the twenty eight things we prayed for, literally overnight.

Which place do you think we liked living in better? One that we searched hard for and was making us sick? Or the one that we believed God for and was 87.5% of what we thought would be our perfect place?

Which of those examples brings God more glory? The one we worked long and hard for and was a mess? Or the one we believed Him for, that showed up the next day, and that was nearly everything we wanted?

The answer is pretty obvious. The more specific we are in our prayers, the more God is glorified when He answers them.

And I will say this. You don't have to write out your prayer requests. While that's worked for us, it's not a formula. At the same time there is real value in writing things down. For one thing, it makes for a powerful testimony when you can remember exactly what you prayed for after that prayer is answered.

The Bible says in Revelation 12:11 that we overcome the enemy by the blood of the Lamb and by the word of our testimony. Making a habit of reviewing what you prayed for and how God answered those prayers, gives you a powerful tool to strengthen your faith.

Throughout the Bible, God regularly told people to build monuments and altars or to write things down to help them remember what God did in the past. Since God is the same yesterday, today, and forever, remembering what He did for you in the past will help boost your faith to see your prayers answered moving forward too.

Also, if you are married, there truly is power when you and your spouse are united on something. To see the power of unity, look at Psalm 133,

> Behold, how good and how pleasant it is
> For brethren to dwell together in unity!
> It is like the precious oil upon the head,
> Running down on the beard,
> The beard of Aaron,
> Running down on the edge of his garments.
> It is like the dew of Hermon,
> Descending upon the mountains of Zion;
> For there the Lord commanded the blessing—
> Life forevermore. — Psalms 133:1-3 (NKJV)

There are blessings throughout the Bible. But there are only four times when God takes it up a level and says that He *commands* a blessing. This is one of those commanded blessings right here where God commands his blessing on unity.

When Lisa and I are united on something, when we lock our hearts together in unity of faith and are truly in agreement on the matter, amazing things happen. If you are married, there is genuine power when you pray in unity with your spouse.

Anyway, after all that we learned what we needed to do as we transitioned overseas. So about six months before we actually arrived in Scotland we sat down and made a list of what we were believing for in our house once we got there. Again, our list wasn't extravagant. But it was specific.

This time we decided we wanted things like off-street parking, and a warm house with good seals around the windows and doors. I think it was just a coincidence that our list for the house in Scotland also had twenty eight things on it.

The house we found after we arrived had twenty seven of the twenty eight things on our list. Our percentage increased to 96% because our faith was growing!

How many houses do you think we had to look at to get one that met those criteria?

We looked at two.

We don't have to travail in the Kingdom of God. Believe it or not, we don't get extra points based on how much effort we put in, or how much we suffer for Jesus. Instead God rewards us based on how well we carry out the assignments he gives us.

Oh, and the last thing on our list? A year after we moved in we were able to get high speed interent because the utility company upgraded their service to our neighborhood.

So today, as I type this, I'm sitting in my office in our house in Scotland that is exactly what we wanted to live in as we move forward in our assignment God has for us here.

There's one more thing you should know about this house. After we moved in, we found out that our landlord had rented it out to someone else. But they backed out on the very same day that we arrived in

Scotland. God truly saved this house just for us.

Every time we tell that story about how God answered the prayers of our house so exactly, God is glorified a little more. We could not have made it work out so quickly and easily, no matter how hard we tried. But it was God's good pleasure to give us this little piece of His Kingdom.

Let me close this section with a couple of bonus scriptures that speak to blessing and stressing.

> *The blessing of the Lord makes one rich,*
> *And He adds no sorrow with it.* — Proverbs 10:22 (NKJV)

We are the blessed of the Lord in Christ. Therefore, God makes us rich without sorrow.

As we mentioned in the first chapter, this is the single biggest difference between the Kingdom of God and the cursed mammon system. Wealth gained via God's ways is baggage free whereas wealth gained from the cursed mammon system has all sorts of negative baggage attached. Mammon hardens hearts and damages relationships, plus a whole lot more.

I find it interesting what the Amplified Classic (AMPC) adds to the end of that verse above: *"neither does toil increase it."* That reminds us that we can't add to God's blessing or try to make it better.

Well we can try. But it's a waste of time. God's blessings are forever perfect just the way He delivers them.

Here's another verse to ponder,

> *It is vain for you to rise early,*
> *To retire late,*
> *To eat the bread of anxious labors —*
> *For He gives [blessings] to His beloved even in his sleep.* — Psalms 127:2 (AMP)

God gives rest to his children. When we're tired all the time it might be because we're trying to accomplish things in our flesh apart from God. That's nothing but wasted effort because God gives sleep to those he loves, which includes you!

Not only does God give you sleep, but He gives you blessings at the same time. I have to regularly remind myself of this. Even though my work is blessed, I am not blessed because of my hard work.

Instead I can go to bed at a decent hour, get plenty of rest, and know that God blesses me and what I do anyway.

The King's Reputation

I want to close out this chapter by talking about the reputation of kings. Remember, the gospel is about the Kingdom of God. Jesus is our King. If you're an American like me, this may be something that isn't obvious to you because we don't have a king in America.

The reputation and wealth of a king is not measured by how much money is in his personal treasury. Instead, it's measured by how prosperous the people in his kingdom are.

We have an example of this in the Bible when the Queen of Sheba goes to visit Solomon. Look at what the Bible says about that visit,

> *And when the queen of Sheba had seen all the wisdom of Solomon, the house that he had built, the food on his table, the seating of his servants, the service of his waiters and their apparel, his cupbearers, and his entryway by which he went up to the house of the Lord, there was no more spirit in her.* — 1 Kings 10:4-5 (NKJV)

What that says is that when the Queen of Sheba saw Solomon's wisdom with her own eyes it literally took her breath away. But what I find most interesting about that passage is how the Bible describes that wisdom.

Solomon's wisdom, and the glory of his kingdom, was displayed in how prosperous his servants were, and how they went about their tasks.

If it was true that Solomon's glory was in how well the people of his kingdom were cared for, how much more is that the case with God?

When you prosper, it reflects well on God. It shows that God is powerful and truly glorious because He takes good care of His people. When we perpetuate a culture of lack, or when we promote mammon's system, we damage God's reputation.

We've already seen how answering our prayers brings Him glory.

> Now this is the confidence that we have in Him, that if we ask anything according to His will, He hears us. And if we know that He hears us, whatever we ask, we know that we have the petitions that we have asked of Him. — 1 John 5:14-15 (NKJV)

It's interesting that John uses the terminology of a courtroom in this passage. He talks about "petitions" and that God "hears" us like in a legal hearing. We know that praying in Jesus' name means we are praying in line with the Kingdom of God.

Therefore when we pray in the name of Jesus, when we pray in line with the Kingdom of God, we are praying something legally in the courts of Heaven and God hears our case. And we know that since God hears us, and since we are in Christ, that God will grant our petitions that we ask of Him.

That's an amazingly powerful scripture about prayer.

Here's another powerful verse about what God gives us,

> Do not be deceived, my beloved brethren. Every good gift and every perfect gift is from above, and comes down from the Father of lights, with whom there is no variation or shadow of turning. — James 1:16-17 (NKJV)

God does *not* send bad things on us. Only good and perfect gifts come from God. It is deception to think otherwise.

It is absolutely vital that you get this truth deep down in your soul. God only sends you good things. If there is something bad in your life, God is *not* the source of that bad thing.

Until we understand that God only sends us good things, we will never be able to have the depth of intimacy with Him that is ours because no one can be truly intimate with someone they think might hurt them at any moment.

Finally, let's close this chapter out with this verse,

> *And my God shall supply all your need according to His riches in glory by Christ Jesus.* — Philippians 4:19 (NKJV)

God supplies all our needs. But the supply isn't based on our need. Instead, God supplies based on His riches.

So when you pray, you don't have to go on and on (and on and on!) about your need. You can just tell God and move on. Focus on His abundance instead of on your lack because that's where your provision will come from.

Chapter 4

Alms: God's Provision for the Poor

*"He who has pity on the poor lends to the Lord,
And He will pay back what he has given."*
— Proverbs 19:17 (NKJV)

The Law of Sowing and Reaping

We've spent three chapters laying a firm foundation. Now we can start building on that foundation by examining practical specifics about how finances work in the Kingdom of God.

Remember, the name of this book is *Rejecting Mammon: How to See Results from Your Giving.* In the rest of this book we are going to talk about the different kinds of giving God put in place in His Kingdom.

But there is one more concept we need to cover before we get to that.

Are you familiar with the law of planting and harvesting, sometimes called sowing and reaping?

The best place to see what we mean by this is in Galatians,

> *Do not be deceived, God is not mocked; for whatever a man sows, that he will also reap. For he who sows to his flesh will of the flesh reap corruption, but he who sows to the Spirit will of the Spirit reap everlasting life.* — Galatians 6:7-8 (NKJV)

Basically, sowing and reaping is a universal law, just like gravity is a universal law. God hardwired it into the universe at creation. We will reap what we sow. Along with other laws that God has put in place, sowing and reaping governs the function of all things natural and supernatural.

There are natural consequences, and spiritual consequences to everything we think, say, and do.

The law of sowing and reaping says you harvest the same exact thing you plant. Like begets like and a seed only produces after its own kind. This means…

- When we plant corn, we harvest corn.

- When we plant tomatoes, we harvest tomatoes.

- An apple seed will never grow into an oak tree.

- When we plant faithfulness, we harvest faithfulness.

- When we plant anger, we will receive more anger from others.

- When we plant forgiveness, we will be forgiven by others.

- The harsh biting words we sow will reap harsh biting words.

- Planting provision for others produces our own harvest of provision.

- When we plant encouragement, we harvest encouragement in our tough times.

- When we sow lies and deceit, we will find others tend to lie to us and deceive us.

I think you get the point.

And I know what some of you are thinking right now. "Oh, no! I better start praying for crop failure!"

While it's true that we always harvest *what* we plant, we often harvest our crop from a different field than we planted. We don't necessarily harvest *where* we plant.

Let me give you an example. When I was a young believer I lived in towns and was part of churches where people moved in and out a fair amount. I made it a habit to help load or unload folk's moving trucks whenever I heard someone needed a hand and I could free my schedule.

Even though I didn't really think about it in these terms at the time, I "sowed" quite a bit of help moving people's homes.

Lisa and I have also moved around a fair amount ourselves. We've always had help moving our furniture every place we've been, even when we hardly knew anyone in whatever new town we moved to.

Because we sowed help moving furniture, we also harvested that same help when we needed it.

But here's the interesting thing about it. We almost never received help from the same people we helped. They had either moved on to another city, or we left them behind when we went to a new town. While we received the same kind of help we offered, that help came from different people.

What that means is we'll always harvest the same crop we sowed. But many times our harvest may come in from a different field than the specific one we planted.

That means we can always be generous with everyone without attaching strings to our generosity and expecting the people we help to somehow owe us. God has already hardwired the law of sowing and reaping into creation. Therefore we will reap what we sow. Just know the harvest will often come in from a different field than the one we planted our seed into.

Since the law of planting and harvesting applies to all things natural and supernatural, do you suppose it applies to money too?

It sure does.

Prosper by Giving

In the Kingdom of God most things work exactly backwards from the way they do in the world. A big example of this is how people prosper under both systems.

In the world's system, the way to prosper is to work hard, acquire and hoard as much as you can. The only way you get anything in the world is if you take it from someone else. And if you're impatient, then why not just borrow the money for what you need? Use your credit card or take out a loan and get it now! You can afford the monthly payments.

In the Kingdom of God, the way to prosper is exactly backwards from that.

> *Give, and it will be given to you: good measure, pressed down, shaken together, and running over will be put into your bosom. For with the same measure that you use, it will be measured back to you.* — Luke 6:38 (NKJV)

In the Kingdom of God, the way to prosper is not to save and hoard. Instead we prosper when we give money away. That makes absolutely no sense whatsoever in the natural.

Look at how the New Living Translation presents that verse.

> *Give, and you will receive. Your gift will return to you in full — pressed down, shaken together to make room for more, running over, and poured into your lap. The amount you give will determine the amount you get back.* — Luke 6:38 (NLT)

When we give in faith, that which we give away will return back to us, in full. In fact, what we receive back is determined by the measure we use when we give. How that actually works is something we will talk about more in chapter eight.

For now, the important part to remember is that the way we prosper in the Kingdom of God is by giving to others.

And this is not just a New Testament principle either. For example, look at this verse in Proverbs,

> *There is one who scatters, yet increases more;*
> *And there is one who withholds more than is right,*
> *But it leads to poverty.* — Proverbs 11:24 (NKJV)

Generosity gets the law of sowing and reaping working in our favor so that we continue to increase even as we give generously to others.

Likewise being stingy and not giving even what is right leads to poverty, and for the same reason. Stingy people put the law of planting and harvesting to work as well, but in the direction of negative results, which ultimately leads to their own poverty.

Look at the next verse there in Proverbs,

> *The generous soul will be made rich,*
> *And he who waters will also be watered himself.* — Proverbs 11:25 (NKJV)

The generous soul will be made rich. He who waters will be watered himself.

That sounds exactly like the law of planting and harvesting, doesn't it. So we can see, when it comes to prospering in both the Old and New Testaments, the key is the same in both: generosity.

The rest of this book, the meat of it really, will cover some specifics on exactly how the Kingdom of God lays out ways for our generosity to prosper us.

We're going to cover five different types of giving that God has spelled out for us in the Bible as part of His Kingdom. We are going to cover the difference between each type of giving in the following areas:

- **Mechanics** — We'll cover how each of these types of giving work. That includes things like how to determine how much to give, where do we give, who should that type of giving be given to, etc.

- **Purpose** — We'll answer the question, what is God's intention within his Kingdom for the different types of giving?

- **Motivation** — We'll address what our heart motivation for each type of giving is so that we are lined up with the Kingdom of God.

- **Promise** — Finally, we'll look at the promise God gives us for each of these different types of giving. These promises are directly tied to how we will prosper as a result of each of these different offerings

Ultimately we are going to see a couple of things as we go through the rest of this material. First, God has put in place a financial system to provide for every need within the Kingdom of God. The other thing we are going to see is that God has also provided the very means we need to prosper financially through these various types of giving.

I don't know about you, but this jazzes me. I get excited about it. When I realized that I can be a part of seeing the Kingdom of God bless people and in the process of participating with that get my own needs met too, I was like, "sign me up! I want a piece of that action!"

Motivation for Giving

There is one more thing I feel is worth bringing up before we go any further. That involves the motivation for our giving.

I see teaching that's all over the map on this point. There are preachers out there that play to the flesh and stir up greed and avarice. They try to turn giving into something mechanical or transactional that is only about what the giver receives.

That's obviously wrong.

On the other extreme I see preachers say that we should never have any intention of receiving anything at all when we give. Instead we should just trust that God will bring it back to us somehow, someway, sometime in the future. That doesn't line up with what I see in the

Bible either.

It's a sticky issue because there likely are people who will misinterpret what I say in this book and try to turn it into a formula even though I explain repeatedly that these Kingdom principles will never work apart from our relationship with God.

I was once in a meeting with a famous preacher who taught an excellent message explaining the way to prosper in the Kingdom of God is through giving. Then towards the end he threw in something along these lines. "But we don't give to get. We only give to bless others."

He spent his whole message up to that point teaching us how to prosper in the Kingdom of God by giving. That's a significant benefit for us to receive. By then going on to say we're wrong if we have a desire to receive God's promises as they relate to giving kind of made the whole thing contradictory.

From my perspective, "giving to get" as that minister said, and "giving to bless others" are not mutually exclusive motivations. We can have the desire for both at the same time. And I think that's OK.

The key thing that will determine whether we move forward in the ways of the Kingdom of God, or we slide down into mammon, is the direction our love flows.

If our love starts to flow towards money and stuff, and we start trying to manipulate others, or even attempt to manipulate God into bringing money our way, then we've lost the plot and our giving is really motivated by mammon.

Paul said it this way,

> And though I bestow all my goods to feed the poor, and though I give my body to be burned, but have not love, it profits me nothing. — 1 Corinthians 13:3 (NKJV)

So if we don't love others in our giving, it profits us nothing. We won't gain anything at all. Likewise, Paul also tells us,

> For the love of money is a root of all kinds of evil, for which some

have strayed from the faith in their greediness, and pierced themselves through with many sorrows. — 1 Timothy 6:10 (NKJV)

Loving money means we are not loving others. That is a very clear picture of what mammon looks like in our lives, along with the detrimental effects that it has on us.

The temptation is to try and remove every bit of motivation and desire to see any increase in our finances as a result of our giving so that we can be sure we aren't sliding into the mammon trap by being guilty of loving money. But that's really just the enemy trying to keep us in poverty. Besides, it won't work.

The more we try to force ourselves not to desire increase, the more we will obsess about money, especially where it concerns how much others have that we don't.

If God has given you a vision to accomplish something and you are on a God-sized assignment, then you will need resources and provision to get it done. Denying you need provision will kill your vision.

Fortunately, the answer to this dilemma is found just a few verses further down in that same chapter. Paul gives us specific instructions to maintain a godly perspective and motivation as we prosper,

> *Command those who are rich in this present age not to be haughty, nor to trust in uncertain riches but in the living God, who gives us richly all things to enjoy. Let them do good, that they be rich in good works, ready to give, willing to share, storing up for themselves a good foundation for the time to come, that they may lay hold on eternal life.* — 1 Timothy 6:17-19 (NKJV)

We aren't to be proud. In the Bible, pride and a haughty spirit is never depicted as a good thing. Pride can take on different forms.

I've seen people who are proud in their giving. They never allow others to bless them. Every single time they insist on paying for the meal, or for coffee, etc. If I have a close enough relationship with them, I will gently remind them that the Kingdom of God works on giving and *receiving*. If they are always giving and never receiving, then they are robbing others of the harvest blessing that would result from sowing into their lives.

It's one thing to be willing to give to others all the time. It's quite another to get proud about it and refuse to allow others to ever bless us. We must both give and receive if we are going to participate in Kingdom ways. I make it a habit to check in with the Holy Spirit first rather than just assume it is my place to pay for everything all the time.

Most times He tells me to follow my desire to bless the people I'm with. But there are times when God replies, "Nope. It's not your time to offer to pay for theirs today." Since I don't know what's going on in the lives and hearts of others, I trust Him to guide me in this.

And I will tell you this. It gets fun when you start hanging out with generous people who understand how the Kingdom works and are always on the lookout for opportunities to sow financially into the lives of others.

When we're like that, we live out Paul's instructions to us in that passage above.

Lisa and I are motivated to give by both a desire to bless others and a desire to see increase in our own lives. You will see what that looks like as you go through the rest of this book.

So let's get to it and see the first type of giving God invites us to participate in.

ALMS

The first type of giving we're going to talk about is by far the most common that we see today. In fact, I'll go so far as to say 99% of all giving both inside and outside the church probably really is this type of giving - that's charitable giving to those in need. The King James Version calls this type of giving "alms".

Some translations translate it as "charitable giving" or "good deeds" or a combination of the two as "charitable deeds". I'm going to use "alms" for the sake of clarity, simply because it is a more specific term.

Alms is the mechanism that God built into His kingdom to provide for the poor.

We see an example of this in Acts chapter three.

> *Now Peter and John went up together to the temple at the hour of prayer, the ninth hour. And a certain man lame from his mother's womb was carried, whom they laid daily at the gate of the temple which is called Beautiful, to ask alms from those who entered the temple; who, seeing Peter and John about to go into the temple, asked for alms.* — Acts 3:1-3 (NKJV)

When we talk about alms, we mean money given to meet a specific need or alleviate suffering. This is the purpose of alms — meeting needs and alleviating suffering.

It is vital that we do this. As children of God citizens of the Kingdom, we have access to the unlimited resources of our Father and our King. When we are generous and give to others to meet their needs and ease their suffering, we reflect our Father's character.

What motivates us to give alms? Compassion. We have compassion on those in need, and those who suffer.

Even the world understands this. That's why they run those emotionally manipulative commercials on TV with the sad music, and the video clips of suffering children, and a professional actor reading a script that is engineered to tug at your compassion, telling you how your three pounds a month will give this child an education that can lift him out of poverty, so that you will text "Help Now" to 099686 with your donation.

Don't get me wrong. The suffering they show in those ads is real. There is a real need to be met there. However, the way they go about sharing that need is manipulative. It targets worldly compassion, and worldly compassion is very different than godly compassion.

Worldly compassion is flesh based. It wants to relieve the suffering, which is a good thing. But, because it is flesh based, it values relieving suffering above the actual person or people who are suffering.

Taken to its extreme, this is how worldly compassion can see euthanasia as a good thing. Worldly compassion sees death as a better option than living with suffering.

Worldly compassion has no problem making a spectacle of the ones in need and how horrible their situation is so that it pulls as hard as possible at the emotions of those who might be in a position to help in order to take as much money as possible from them.

Worldly compassion is OK with bragging about how much they give to the poor because it showcases about all the different needs being met and all the different people being helped.

That's not how God operates. Godly compassion values each individual as a whole above any part of that individual. Yes, godly compassion desires to relieve suffering. But godly compassion doesn't see death as more desirable to life, even when suffering is involved.

God never humiliates people in order to bless them. Any theology that claims He does, is out of touch with God's true character. He always protects their dignity and honors individuals.

This is why Jesus was so adamant that we should never talk specifically about our alms giving. When we give to meet a need, or alleviate suffering, we should keep that to ourselves.

> *Take heed that you do not do your charitable deeds before men, to be seen by them. Otherwise you have no reward from your Father in heaven. Therefore, when you do a charitable deed, do not sound a trumpet before you as the hypocrites do in the synagogues and in the streets, that they may have glory from men. Assuredly, I say to you, they have their reward. But when you do a charitable deed, do not let your left hand know what your right hand is doing, that your charitable deed may be in secret; and your Father who sees in secret will Himself reward you openly.* — Matthew 6:1-4 (NKJV)

Remember, we said that "charitable deeds" is one of the phrases modern translations use for "alms." Jesus would never parade people in need across the television screen to raise money for them. Jesus has true godly compassion, and that compassion will always protect the dignity of those being assisted.

In fact, Jesus went so far as to say that it's vital we give our alms secretly. Otherwise we miss out on the promised reward God has for us when we give alms.

What is that promise?

Look at Proverbs 19:17,

> *He who has pity on the poor lends to the Lord,*
> *And He will pay back what he has given.* — Proverbs 19:17 (NKJV)

Remember the power of promises. This is something we can believe and therefore act on in faith, right?

Is this an unconditional promise? Or is it conditional?

There's a condition. In order to receive the promise we must first have pity on the poor by giving to relieve their suffering. It says that when we give our alms to those in need, that's a loan to God Himself, as far as the Kingdom of God is concerned. And it says God will pay back whatever we give.

That's a one-to-one return on our "investment". Let me ask you this. How much profit is that? Nothing. But we'll get it all back. It's like we give God a zero percent loan whenever we give alms.

If you truly believed that everything you gave away you would get returned to you, how would that affect your willingness to give to others?

Now remember, Jesus said there's a catch. Jesus said that if we don't give our alms in secret so that we protect the dignity of those we are assisting, then the only reward we get is from other people. When we tell others about our alms, we forfeit our right to that promise and God is no longer obligated to repay. In that case God gives us nothing as a result of that giving.

I want to point out something else. The giving of alms is the *only* type of giving that Jesus put this kind of restriction on when it comes to talking about it.

Before we're done with this book we're going examine four more types of giving. Jesus didn't say anything about not talking about any of those other types of giving. We can talk about those other types of giving all day long because doing so brings glory to God.

But we should never talk about our alms giving, because that humiliates the very people those alms were meant to assist. Not to mention it disqualifies us from receiving the promised repayment for our giving.

Unfortunately the world, and pretty much the overwhelming majority of Christians, get this exactly backwards. They talk all about how much they are doing for the poor, to meet people's need and alleviate suffering. But they rarely if ever mention the other ways they give money.

Of course most of them probably aren't giving any other way anyway.

How does "not talking about your alms" look in a practical sense?

Let's say, hypothetically, I headed up a business and was presented with an opportunity to donate some toys for a toy appeal at Christmas time. Let's say, hypothetically, our staff decided this is something we wanted to be involved with as an organization. We saw some children in need, were moved by compassion, and wanted to donate toys to this cause.

If that were to happen then, hypothetically, here's how it should play out.

We can talk about it internally within our office. We can discuss it as a staff.

In the case of our hypothetical business, we're part of an organization that involves multiple people. If we didn't talk about it internally amongst ourselves, then how would the toys ever get donated?

And if any money comes out of the business, then we obviously need to keep accurate records of that and we would need to inform our accounting department about it. Again, that's an internal conversation which is required for the donation to happen properly and legally.

However, now let's say, in this hypothetical situation, that the management that owns the property our business rented were the folks that made us aware of this toy drive and they are collecting toys centrally for all the various tenants on their properties, including us. And let's say they did something like ask us to attend a photo shoot so they could get a photo of all of their tenants who donated toys.

According to Jesus, that photo shoot is something we should politely decline to participate in. We don't have to get preachy or judgmental and say, "That's wrong!" Instead we can just politely say, "we prefer to donate anonymously, and would prefer not to be in the photo."

Think about it. In the world's system that the property management company operates in, talking about your charity work is perfectly acceptable. But we are citizens of a different kingdom. So even though talking about our alms giving is something our Kingdom culture doesn't do, we have no business pushing that cultural norm of the Kingdom onto people who are citizens of another culture outside the Kingdom.

This right here could open up a whole other discussion about the cultural things of the Kingdom that we can get obnoxious about with the world. In my opinion, as someone who moved from America to Scotland, there are cultural differences that are very real. But I don't go around preaching at Scots telling them to change their culture. Think about how obnoxious I would be if I brought driving on the other side of the road into every conversation. Constantly going around telling everyone here that they really should be driving on the other side of the road, because after all the side they drive on here is obviously not the right side, would repel people. Besides, it's silly.

So much of what Christians get so mean and critical about with the world is cultural, or at least it should be. Kingdom culture should be different. When people ask, we can have conversations about it and share what those differences are and why those things are done differently in the Kingdom of God.

But trying to get the world to conform to the culture of the Kingdom of God is unlikely to be any more fruitful than trying to get Scots to start driving on the right side of the road.

But I tell you what. When a Scotsman moves to America, when he changes from one kingdom to another, he will start driving on the right side of the road pretty much immediately. Likewise when someone is born again and enters the Kingdom of God, that is when we start teaching them on Kingdom ways. It's called discipleship.

Anyway, in the situation about donating the toys, we just politely decline to be in the photo. Also, we should not post on Facebook that we gave a bunch of toys. Nor should we put it on our website, or in our company newsletter that we did.

In our hypothetical case, a toy appeal is not our primary mission. That means, in this case, donating toys would be part of our alms giving. Therefore, according to Jesus, we should not be talking about it to other folks. It doesn't matter that we don't know which particular child received the specific toy we donated.

We choose to follow the instructions Jesus gave us and not say anything. At the same time we lock our faith into God's promise that he will repay whatever alms we donate to help meet a need.

So, to review, when we are talking about Alms:

What is Alms? Money given to a specific need or to alleviate suffering

Who is it given to? Anyone in need, either believer or unbeliever.

Motivation: Compassion, which is why we don't talk about our alms

Promise: one for one replacement of what was given

Key Scripture: Proverbs 19:17

> *He who has pity on the poor lends to the Lord, and He will pay back what he has given.*

Also: Jesus added a further requirement to this conditional promise, that we do not talk about our alms giving. Why did He do that? To protect the dignity of the people being assisted and honor them.

Is It Alms?

How do you know if your giving is alms? This is an important question. Many people think they are sowing seed, when they are really giving alms instead.

Obviously you can see that would be a problem, right?

If you think you are sowing seed and are expecting a thirty, sixty, or hundredfold harvest on your giving, but you are actually giving alms, what's going to happen?

God only promises a one-to-one return on our alms. So someone looking for a seed harvest from alms is going to be pretty disappointed, aren't they?

That's especially true if they go blabbing all over the place about their giving. When they do that, they disqualify themselves from even seeing their giving come back to them, according to what Jesus said.

Talk about messing with someones expectations!

Then they may very well conclude this giving thing doesn't work. When the truth is the problem is not with God's system, but rather with their understanding of how God's system works.

So how do you know if you're giving alms?

Look at your motivation. If compassion is rising up and you want to help meet a specific need, that's alms.

Planting financial seed looks totally different. And we're going to talk about that in chapter eight.

Chapter 5

The Tithe: Protecting What God Has Given Us

"Bring all the tithes into the storehouse,
That there may be food in My house,
And try Me now in this,"
Says the Lord of hosts,
"If I will not open for you the windows of heaven
And pour out for you such blessing
That there will not be room enough to receive it.
And I will rebuke the devourer for your sakes,
So that he will not destroy the fruit of your ground,
Nor shall the vine fail to bear fruit for you in the field,"
Says the Lord of hosts;
— Malachi 3:10-11 (NKJV)

The Law of Firstfruits

In this chapter we are going to look at the tithe. Today the tithe is as controversial in grace circles as praying in tongues is in some Christian circles. I believe the roots of the controversy are exactly the same for both tongues and the tithe: the enemy knows what powerful weapons these are in the hands of believers. Therefore he does everything he can to keep believers from benefitting from using those weapons against him.

As we know, when we pray in tongues our spirit bypasses our flesh and the words come out pure and powerful, uncorrupted by any junk that might be in our souls. Praying in tongues also builds us up as believers (1 Corinthians 14:4).

That makes tongues a very powerful weapon against the schemes of the enemy.

As we will see, the tithe is arguably the strongest weapon we have against the enemy in the area of our finances. There is an incredibly powerful promise associated with the tithe regarding our finances that is not found anywhere else in scripture.

Before we get to that we need to talk about another universal law found in the Kingdom of God - the Law of Firstfruits.

In Romans chapter 11 Paul talks about how Israel rejected Jesus and that rejection opened the door of salvation to the Gentiles. One of God's purposes in bringing us Gentiles into his Kingdom is provoking the Jews to jealousy, and thereby saving some of them.

In the middle of this discourse Paul says something very interesting in verse 16,

> For if the firstfruit is holy, the lump is also holy; and if the root is holy, so are the branches. — Romans 11:16 (NKJV)

There was a firstfruits offering in the Old Covenant. And actually we're going to talk about the firstfruits offering in the next chapter when we'll explore how it applies to us today as citizens of the Kingdom of God.

But this verse is something different because Paul states it as a straight-forward universal law.

What does it mean to make something holy?

In this case it means to dedicate it to the Lord, to set it apart as a special possession of God.

In this verse Paul says that holiness can be imparted on something a couple different ways. If the roots of something are set apart as a special possession of God, then everything that springs from that root will also have that same holiness in its core.

At the same time, this verse also says that when we dedicate a portion of something to God, the rest of that thing also takes on that same holiness.

We're going to see how this law of firstfruits applies to the tithe here in a moment.

Tithe Defined

The word tithe simply means *a tenth part*. And that's what the tithe is. The tithe is an offering of a tenth, or 10% of our income to God. What we do when we tithe is give ten percent of our income into the Kingdom of God.

When we tithe, we honor God and recognize Him as the source of all our provision because we are giving him the first tenth of all that comes to us. The very act of tithing goes a long way towards protecting us from the love of money creeping into our hearts because it prioritizes God above our money.

Remember there are two financial systems. Even though money is a creation of the earth's cursed mammon system, it turns out that it's possible for us to move our money out of that system and into the Kingdom of God.

One of the primary ways we move our money across and into the Kingdom is via the tithe. It does this because of the Law of Firstfruits. By giving that first 10% into the Kingdom of God, we make that bit of our money holy.

And since that first part of our income that we donate is made holy, then all the rest of our income becomes holy too. In this way our money is then spiritually transferred out of the mammon system and into the Kingdom of God.

Guess which system has more opportunity to see the hand of God's blessing operate in our finances? Obviously the answer to that question is within God's own Kingdom.

Where, specifically, do we give our tithes? I've heard some Bible teachers say that we should tithe where we are fed. Personally, Lisa and I give our tithes to the local church. The way I see it, there are 4 other types of giving that give me ways to participate in other ministries. Therefore we commit our tithes to the local church.

But here's the thing. According to Hebrews chapter 7, it is Jesus who receives our tithes. Since Jesus is the head of the church, I'm comfortable giving Him our own tithes via our local church.

We're under grace, so you can check in with the Holy Spirit and let Him guide you on where to tithe, whether it's the local church or somewhere else. The most important thing is that our tithes need to go into the Kingdom of God. That way we give them to Jesus and move the rest of our money into the Kingdom too, because of the law of firstfruits.

Tithing Before the Law

The first time we see the word tithe in the Bible is in Genesis chapter 14. If you remember the story, Abram (before God changed his name to Abraham) went to battle against five kings to get his nephew Lot back from captivity. Abram was victorious. Not only did he get Lot and his family back, but he also got all the spoils of war that the five kings had captured.

Then we see this curious incident starting in verse 18,

> Then Melchizedek king of Salem brought out bread and wine; he was the priest of God Most High. And he blessed him and said:
>
> "Blessed be Abram of God Most High,
> Possessor of heaven and earth;

> *And blessed be God Most High,*
> *Who has delivered your enemies into your hand." And he gave him a*
> *tithe of all.* — Genesis 14:18-20 (NKJV)

We don't really know much about Melchizedek. The only time he shows up in history is in these three verses in Genesis 14. He's only mentioned one other time in the Old Testament, in Psalms 110,

> *The Lord has sworn*
> *And will not relent,*
> *"You are a priest forever*
> *According to the order of Melchizedek."* — Psalms 110:4 (NKJV)

What's interesting is that most of what we know about Melchizedek comes from the New Testament in the Book of Hebrews. There he's actually flat-out equated to Jesus. The writer of Hebrews quotes that verse in Psalms 110:4 at least five times in chapters five through seven as he establishes the case for the eternal priesthood of Jesus.

Hebrews makes it very clear that David's Psalm 110 was written prophetically about Jesus. That makes sense, because Jesus actually referred to that same Psalm Himself in Matthew 22:44 when the Pharisees were trying to trap Him in issues about the Law.

But my point here is that Abraham tithed from the spoils of his victory to Melchizedek, a priest of the Most High God. Hebrews 7:2 reiterates that Abraham gave a tenth of the spoils.

The Bible is clear that Abraham gave him a tenth of everything he gained. That included all the agricultural spoils — animals and whatnot — as well as all the monetary spoils he gained too.

There is no place in the Bible that we see where Abraham was instructed by God to tithe. As far as we can see Abraham did it of his own free will and initiative. And remember, this was long before the Old Testament Law was put in place.

If you notice in that passage from Genesis 14, not only does it say that Melchizedek is a priest of the Most High God, it also says, "Blessed be Abram of the God Most High." Both of these guys belonged to God's Kingdom. Abraham could have tithed to anyone, at least in theory. But he gave that offering to a recognized man of God.

All that to say, this really is the example we have in scripture as our basis for tithing today for two reasons.

First, as believers and followers of Jesus, the Bible says that we are blessed along with believing Abraham (Galatians 3:9). Then it goes on to say this:

> Christ has redeemed us from the curse of the law, having become a curse for us (for it is written, "Cursed is everyone who hangs on a tree"), that the blessing of Abraham might come upon the Gentiles in Christ Jesus, **that we might receive the promise of the Spirit through faith.** — Galatians 3:13-14 (NKJV)

That very clearly says that as followers of Jesus we share in the same blessings as Abraham, and that same faith entitles us to receive God's promises.

The other reason why this incident with Melchizedek is our model is because Jesus is our High Priest according to the order of Melchizedek. This is the main thrust of that passage in Hebrews that talks about Melchizedek. There it plainly says that Jesus is not in the line of Aaron. He's not a levitical priest. That section of Hebrews makes the case that Jesus is part of an even better priestly line.

Those two facts, that we share in Abraham's blessing and promises, and that Jesus is a priest according the order of Melchizedek make this example in Genesis the precedent for us to follow when tithing in the New Covenant.

Abraham represents us. Melchizedek represents Jesus. Abraham tithed from the abundance that God gave him to Melchizedek, the priest and king, as an example for us in tithing from the abundance God gives us to our own High Priest and King Jesus.

TITHING IN THE LAW

Of course there's no denying that the tithe was part of the Law. God set up very specific criteria for how the people were supposed to tithe under the Old Covenant.

Actually the Law contains at least three different tithes. They all have different instructions about how they were supposed to be given, what they were supposed to be used for, and so on.

But here's the thing. I'm not going to go into all that right now because we're not under the Law, we're under grace. We don't need to get wrapped around the axle with all the details of tithing under the law when we want to be tithing in faith instead anyway, right?

Even so, it is important to know that God included tithing as part of the Old Covenant.

Remember I said earlier that tithing is pretty controversial? That seems to be especially the case for folks in grace circles. One of the big stumbling blocks is that they only see tithing as a Law thing and get hung up there.

Yes, it is part of the Law. But it also very much is available for us to tap into by faith today as part of our New Covenant of grace.

Main Reasons Given for Not Tithing

I feel pretty passionate about this particular issue because I see how much it holds people back from stepping into the financial inheritance God intends for them to experience. Therefore I have been known to wade into Facebook discussions and whatnot from time to time when the subject of the tithe comes up.

I sincerely try not to go there. But hey, I'm a work in progress. So every now and then I wade into a discussion anyway.

One good thing to come out of it is that I've seen a whole lot of the arguments and teaching that's out there trying to prevent believers from tithing.

I even see people who say that Jesus is the tithe. Therefore, they claim that the concept of believers tithing has no meaning anymore because they see it as redundant. I've looked at their exegesis and I'm not seeing it. At all.

When I look at the scriptures those folk use in context, I come to a very different conclusion. To me that seems to be a classic case of starting with an idea and then searching the Bible to try and find verses to "prove" the initial statement. When I set aside my preconceived ideas and let scripture interpret scripture I come to a very different conclusion.

Generally speaking most all the objections people have with the tithe seem to fall into three overarching categories:

1. We're under grace instead of the Law, therefore we *shouldn't* tithe.

Because the tithe is included in the Law, some people get all distracted with the legalities of who gets the tithe, how to translate the tithe from an agrarian economy to an post-industrial economy, and whatnot. But all that misses the point. Tithing is a heart issue. It's putting God first in our finances and recognizing Him as the source of our provision. It's about boldness in faith that God will fulfill His promise that He made as it relates to our finances.

Many folks seem to think there are only two options where the tithe is concerned - tithe under the Law, or not tithe at all. However, there is a third option - tithing in faith under grace. Since we can choose not to tithe bound to the Law, all the blah, blah, blah about who gets the tithe, how to translate the tithe from an agrarian economy to our post-industrial currency based economy, and so on, is just a distraction.

Yes, it is very true that we are no longer under the Law. Therefore we should not be tithing legalistically.

We're going to explore what it means to tithe under grace and in faith. I think then you'll see how different that is from tithing legalistically.

Then you get to decide if you want to participate in God's Kingdom that way or not. As we will see before we're done with this chapter, you truly do have the freedom to choose.

2. I give more than 10% therefore I *don't* tithe.

This one seems so silly to me that I hesitate to bring it up. Unfortunately I encounter this objection to tithing quite a bit. And until I did run into people who said just this, it never occurred to me that someone would think that if they tithed then they were somehow prohibited from giving anything else beyond that.

What really amazes me is how tightly people hold to this strange idea even after I point out to them that it is very possible to tithe and give more over and above the amount tithed. In fact, that's not a problem at all. Even after explaining that, I have actually gone round and round with people who just can't seem to grasp it.

The truth is, anyone who participates fully in giving the way God set it up in His Kingdom will probably end up giving away somewhere in the 20 - 30% range, at least. Granted, very few people start giving at those levels. But as folks grow in this area to where they participate fully in the Kingdom, that's where they will likely end up.

As an example, Lisa and I do participate in all these types of Kingdom giving we cover in this book. The year we arrived in Scotland we gave 23% of our income away to various charitable causes. I only know that number because we need to track that number for our taxes back in America. That number doesn't count things like buying coffee or a meal for friends when we're out, or other gifts we give to folks "just because." It was just what we gave to officially recognized charities. And that was the year we transitioned overseas as missionaries!

Now I don't throw that number out to try and impress anyone because I'm sure there are many people who give away much higher percentages of their income.

My point is simply this. We tithe faithfully. (And we tithe in faith, too. Those aren't necessarily the same thing.) At the same time, by participating in the other forms of giving that God put in place we manage to give well over twice that amount overall to charity.

Someone who thinks that tithing somehow limits what they can give needs to get a revelation! That's some serious stinkin' thinkin' right there!

Not only can we give more than our tithe, we absolutely should give more! Citizens of the Kingdom of God should be generous. We are called to be like our Father in heaven. He gave His only begotten Son, that we might have life. If we are tithing, then we should also want to participate in other forms of giving too!

3. There are manipulative pastors out there who teach the tithe wrongly, therefore I *won't* tithe.

I get that there are a whole bunch of ministers out there today who use abusive faulty teaching on the tithe to manipulate and control people. There are fearful, greedy, self-indulgent ministers out there who abuse people for financial gain. I get that.

But let's see that for what it is. Those ministers are caught up in the earth cursed Babylonian system of mammon.

We need to be honest. There are people who teach all kinds of wacky manipulative, controlling things when it comes to salvation too, as just another example. Maybe you've experienced some of that.

In fact, you can pick any subject that Jesus taught about, or that we see on the pages of the New Testament, and even core doctrines of the church, and there will be some people teaching kookooluna craziness about it instead of the truth.

Would we even consider setting aside salvation because there are preachers out there trying to manipulate people into saying a sinners prayer for their own selfish gain?

I think we would more likely show compassion towards that person who was abused and say, "Look. I'm sorry that other minister treated you so badly. That wasn't a good representation of Jesus. Here's the truth when it comes to salvation."

If we will obviously do that with salvation, why wouldn't we also do the same thing when it comes to the tithe?

Please know that I am in no way minimizing how hurtful being manipulated by others can be.

In fact, I am truly sorry if someone has used faulty teaching on the tithe to abuse, manipulate, or control you. As an ambassador of the Kingdom of God, representing King Jesus, I sincerely apologize for that misrepresentation of how we citizens of Heaven living here on earth do things. The way you were treated was wrong. Please know, that did not accurately portray how we operate in God's Kingdom.

I encourage you to take all the pain from that hurtful experience and put it on the cross. Jesus is waiting to take that pain from you, if you will only give it to Him. In return He offers His healing and wholeness. It's a simple exchange, available to you right now, if you are willing to accept it by faith.

If you've given up on tithing because of abusive ministers, please be encouraged. There is no pressure here. I'm going to share a few more truths with you about tithing, and then you get to decide if you want to tithe or not.

Law of Love

The truth is this: In the New Covenant, there is no law in the Old Covenant sense, save the law of love. Therefore there is no compulsion to tithe. Believers absolutely are free not to tithe.

Please hear me in this. As a believer and follower of Jesus Christ, there is absolutely no requirement any more to tithe. There is no longer any curse for not tithing as there was under the Old Covenant.

As a believer, you are absolutely free to choose not to tithe. As a New Testament believer you are **not** robbing God if you don't tithe.

Now. I want to make sure you understand this point. What did I just say?

Believers today do not have to tithe.

Let me check one more time to see if you got that. Do you have to tithe today? No!

OK. Now that we have established that, I will say this. It is *my opinion* that, knowing what I know about the tithe and how effective the promise associated with the tithe is at keeping the enemy out of our personal finances, I would be unwise to ever stop my own tithing.

I don't have to tithe at all. There is no curse if I don't tithe. At the same time, there is no promise if I don't tithe either. It's purely my choice to receive the promise we're going to talk about in a moment by meeting the condition God put on that promise by tithing.

Tithing in faith is what I choose to do. Likewise, you have the freedom to choose for yourself whether or not you will tithe.

The Promise of the Tithe

So what is this promise? Listen to what God Himself says about the tithe in Malachi chapter 3,

> *Bring all the tithes into the storehouse,*
> *That there may be food in My house,*
> *And try Me now in this,"*
> *Says the Lord of hosts,*
> *"If I will not open for you the windows of heaven*
> *And pour out for you such blessing*
> *That there will not be room enough to receive it.*
> *And I will rebuke the devourer for your sakes,*
> *So that he will not destroy the fruit of your ground,*
> *Nor shall the vine fail to bear fruit for you in the field,"*
> *Says the Lord of hosts;* — Malachi 3:10-11 (NKJV)

There are two promises in these verses. First question. Are these promises unconditional or conditional?

They are conditional. Verse 10 starts by saying our part is to bring our tithes to God. Once we do that, then the promises are available to us.

What are those promises?

1. **God will open the windows of heaven and pour out such a blessing that there will not be room enough to receive it.**

That's a pretty powerful blessing. Though to be fair, there are tons of blessings piled all through scripture. And none of those other blessings have anything to do with the tithe.

So you absolutely are blessed based on all those other scriptures even if you do not tithe.

2.   God will rebuke the devourer for our sake.

This promise is different. I don't see a promise like this anywhere else in the Bible.

First, we need to figure out what the devourer is. In context this verse is literally talking about crops being protected from insects and disease. Do you think this passage might have any relevance to us today? Or should we throw it out because we don't live in an agrarian society anymore?

That Hebrew word that the New King James translates as devourer can mean insects or pestilence. It absolutely can. And some translations say just that. The word means *to eat, burn up, or consume like a flame; to waste away.*

What do crops represent to a farmer? Crops are a farmer's income, right? He's going to sell the harvest in order to purchase other things he needs for his life.

Therefore, we can clearly say that the devourer is anything that eats, consumes, burns up, or wastes away our income. Do you know what the devourer looks like in a practical sense?

Any time you get an unexpected bill that is outside your normal monthly budget — like say a doctor's bill, an unexpected car repair, or a tax bill — that's the devourer moving in on your finances.

Think about it. In some respects, it really doesn't matter how much money you have coming in the front door. If the vault you are storing your money in has a huge hole in it so the money is draining out faster than you can put more money in, you are not going to prosper no matter how much you more you bring in the front door.

Life happens. We all get unexpected expenses that pop up from time to time. In Malachi 3:11 God says that when we tithe, He will personally rebuke the devourer for our sakes.

We don't have to do the rebuking. We just have to stand in faith, and remind God of His promise.

And it's not like He forgets, either. "Oh, did I promise to do that? I don't remember."

No. That's not it at all. What needs to happen is for us to stand in faith. Remember what James says. *"Submit to God. Resist the devil and he will flee from you"* (James 4:7).

We submit to God. When we pray God's word back to Him, when we remind God of the promises He has made to us, that is an excellent way to submit to Him. "God, I'm following your word. I'm standing on it. You said that you would rebuke the devourer for my sake because I tithe. This unexpected bill just came in. I really need you to deal with it like you promised you would."

Then watch what happens.

Time and time again, my wife and I have seen those unexpected bills reduce to nearly nothing, or even better. But before we get to some testimonies, let's review the tithe.

What is the tithe? Offering of 10% of our income to Jesus which funds the local church and work of ministers.

Who is it given to? Usually our local church, or as Jesus directs us.

Motivation: Obedience, to move our finances out of the mammon system into the Kingdom of God, and to meet the conditions of God's promise.

Promise: God opens the windows of Heaven to pour out so much to us we will have trouble receiving it all and He will rebuke the devourer for our sake to protect against unforeseen loss.

Key Scripture: Malachi 3:10-11

> *Bring all the tithes into the storehouse,*
> *That there may be food in My house,*

> *And try Me now in this,"*
> *Says the Lord of hosts,*
> *"If I will not open for you the windows of heaven*
> *And pour out for you such blessing*
> *That there will not be room enough to receive it.*
> *And I will rebuke the devourer for your sakes,*
> *So that he will not destroy the fruit of your ground,*
> *Nor shall the vine fail to bear fruit for you in the field,"*
> *Says the Lord of hosts;*

Tithe Testimonies

This is an incredibly powerful promise for us to lock our faith into so we can see supernatural results in our finances. What I do whenever we have an unexpected bill come our way is this. I remind God that we tithe and ask Him to keep His promise to rebuke the devourer for our sake with that car repair (or other bill). Time and time again Lisa and I have seen those bills go down to nearly nothing if they don't disappear entirely.

For example, before we left America we had a 1998 Ford Taurus and a 2003 Jeep Grand Cherokee. They were older cars, sure. But they had always been reliable over the years we owned them. Besides, I worked from home so that Taurus had really low mileage for a car of its age.

About six months before we left we started hearing a squeak coming from what sounded like the back end of the Jeep. I'm not mechanically inclined but my best guess was there was something wrong with the brakes. Two different mechanics were not able to fix it. The second shop told me it was in the transmission. They even brought me back into the garage with the car on the lift and showed me that it sounded like it was coming from the transmission when the drive shaft was turned manually.

To fix/replace the transmission would have been like a $1500 - $2000 repair. Keep in mind we were working on saving money to get to the mission field at that point. So we had much better uses for that money. I was frustrated about the bill we were looking at when Lisa put her foot down. She said, "*No! This is not going to be an expensive repair because we tithe!"*

At that moment I repented and came into agreement with her and with the Word of God.

The next day we took it to a transmission shop. Turns out there was nothing wrong with our transmission. Our brakes really did need some sort of adjustment. The transmission shop did that for us and the total bill was $70.

Seventy dollars was no problem at all for us, especially compared to the total expense we were looking at in that case! Since then our belief in the power of the tithe has grown significantly and I've got more testimonies.

The whole story of the car we are driving right now is so amazing I had to really get with God so He could explain to me how that happened.

Here's what I believe the Holy Spirit said to me. Our current car came to us as a direct result of the fact that we tithe faithfully, and in faith.

This isn't the first car we've owned since we moved to Scotland. Before we moved here some friends felt impressed by God to give us their older car. That was a tremendous blessing for us! We were mobile from the moment we hit the ground and saved a significant amount of money that would have otherwise been spent on both renting and then buying a car.

We hadn't been here quite a year when I followed the blue line on Google Maps and foolishly drove that first little Citroën down a tractor path that I had no business being on. In the process I managed to tear out the exhaust so it was dragging on the ground and punctured the oil pan sump. All the oil drained out when we parked it. And there were some other things that were messed up too. (Did I mention I'm not mechanically inclined?)

The estimate to fix the whole thing was nearly four times what the car was worth! Needless to say, that was an unexpected bill.

Plus, the whole thing was totally my fault.

But that didn't matter to God. He cracked a window of Heaven open anyway. He prompted Lisa to ask me to call about this insurance letter we got a few months before I messed up the car.

Turns out there was over $16,000 sitting in an account that we didn't even know we had. I opened that account 28 years earlier, then forgot all about it. Despite the fact that I was rather irresponsible with my money when I was younger, God had me set up the whole thing so that it just sat there and grew until the opportune time. It was enough to pay cash for a lightly used, larger, newer, nicer car.

The devourer tried to use my ignorance and misplaced trust in Google Maps against us to come at our finances with a huge unexpected bill. Because we tithe, God rebuked him, and cracked a window of Heaven and blessed us with the nicest car Lisa and I have ever owned, paid for in full.

The key here is to understand what the promise is and stand on that in faith. The enemy may very well try and steal that promise from you. Don't let yourself slide into fear and give the enemy an opening when that unexpected bill first shows up. Stay in peace.

Lisa and I were laughing when we got out of the car and saw what I'd done to it. Rather than freak out about the damage I caused, we laughed at what a stupid decision I made to drive up that path.

To be perfectly honest, it was kind of fun driving like a true rally car racer trying to make it through that mess. I knew if I stopped at any point we were going to need to find someone with a tractor to pull us out.

One of the first things Lisa said when we got out of the car was, "God, you've got a problem." And she was right. In order to accomplish the things God assigned us to do here in Scotland, we need transportation. We're on His assignment, so really it was His problem.

And He solved it in a way that seemed down right miraculous to us because He had me set aside the money we needed 28 years earlier and then completely forget about it until that letter came in. Let me point out that we'd been married over twenty years at that point. Lisa does our books and she had never even heard of that company until that letter arrived. I've moved many times and lived in at least five different states in the twenty eight years since I opened that account.

Yet somehow, that letter found us right when we needed it. I can't explain that apart from God.

And let me add this. Please don't think you need to have a ton of money before you can start tithing. I started tithing when I was unemployed.

Back then I didn't know much of anything about what I've shared in this chapter. But I did see that bit there in those verses where God said, *"test me in this!"*

So I did.

Since God knew how much money I needed anyway, I told Him that I would start tithing and He was going to have to bring in what I needed to cover my bills, plus 10% to cover the tithe too, even though I was unemployed. I figured if He didn't hold up his end then I could stop tithing at any time. Turns out God's always been true to His word. The money came in. Go figure!

That was over 20 years ago.

And now that I understand how the tithe really works on our behalf, and have experienced the benefits of those promises first hand, I can't imagine ever stopping!

Let's close out this chapter with this one thought to sum up:

When we tithe we move our money out of the world's cursed mammon system into the Kingdom where God can legally bless and protect it.

Chapter 6

Firstfruits: Keeping the Storehouse Full

"Honor the Lord with your possessions,
And with the firstfruits of all your increase;
So your barns will be filled with plenty,
And your vats will overflow with new wine."
— Proverbs 3:9-10 (NKJV)

Law of Firstfruits

In this chapter we will look at the firstfruits offering. The firstfruits offering is distinct from the Law of Firstfruits that we mentioned earlier. And like the tithe, the firstfruits offering also ties into the Law of Firstfruits.

Because these three concepts are all related, it can get a little confusing for folks sometimes. Hopefully by the end of this chapter you will understand the differences and it will all make sense to you.

Again, keep in mind that we're not in any way obligated to give our money in any of the different ways we are talking about in this book.

God will not curse us if we choose not to give any of these offerings.

All we are doing is looking at the promises God makes available for us to tap into by faith. None of this is a formula. You will not see Kingdom results outside of your personal relationship with Jesus the King.

Before we get to the meat of this chapter, let's review the Law of Firstfruits.

If you remember, in the last chapter we said that Paul reveals something very interesting in Romans 11:16,

> For if the firstfruit is holy, the lump is also holy; and if the root is holy, so are the branches.

Paul states this as a straight-forward universal law.

Do you remember what it means to make something holy?

In this case it means to dedicate it to the Lord, to set it apart as a special possession of God.

In this verse Paul says that holiness — dedicating something to the Lord as His special possession — can be imparted on something when we dedicate a portion of something to God; the rest of that thing also takes on that same holiness.

It is because of this spiritual Law of Firstfruits that tithing gives God the a legal right to bless and protect our finances. When we take a portion of our income and dedicate it to the Lord — in the case of the tithe the portion is 10% — then the Law of Firstfruts causes all the money we earn to effectively be moved from the world's mammon system into the Kingdom of God.

Now that we understand the Law of Firstfruits, let's take a look at the firstfruit offering and it's application to us as New Covenant believers.

The key scripture for us when we talk about the firstfruit offering is Proverbs 3:9-10,

> Honor the Lord with your possessions,

And with the firstfruits of all your increase;
So your barns will be filled with plenty,
And your vats will overflow with new wine.

Honoring God

The first thing I want to point out in this passage is that the focus of this offering is our relationship with God and honoring Him. This is true of all our offerings. But this is a good reminder for us.

Remember, we are talking about financial principles found within the Kingdom of God. The Kingdom has a King. As we all know, His name is Jesus.

This is something that can be a bit challenging for most Americans to get our heads around. America doesn't have a king. In fact, America was birthed as the result of a war that was fought specifically to disconnect from a king.

As an American citizen, the President is not my lord. He's also subject to our constitution and laws just as I am as a private citizen. Well, at least in theory anyway.

Even where I currently live in the United Kingdom where there is still a monarchy, the Queen's rule is not absolute. I'm not well versed in the British constitutional system. But from what I understand the Queen must work with Parliament to establish laws and rule the nation.

The Kingdom of God is different. Jesus is the absolute authority in His Kingdom. In fact, we can go a step further and say that Jesus *is* the Kingdom. Because without the King, there is no Kingdom.

This is really what distinguishes the Kingdom of God from religion. Most religious people will say that the King is in charge. But then religious people want to argue about what He says, apply creative interpretations, or even change it outright.

That's not how a Kingdom works.

The King is the final authority in his Kingdom, full stop. This is one of the reasons the way Jesus taught was so different from what people were used to seeing. Jesus didn't refer to another authority.

All of the Gospel accounts make note of Jesus' authority. Here's one example,

> *And they were astonished at His teaching, for He taught them as one having authority, and not as the scribes.* — Mark 1:22 (NKJV)

The Kingdom's authority rests solely in the King. Therefore everything we do within the Kingdom of God must necessarily flow out of our relationship with the King.

If you try to turn this giving stuff into some sort of formula or procedure without honoring God, then you are basically turning it into nothing more than a religious system. All of our giving flows from our relationship with Jesus and with the Father. That's the only way we will see Kingdom results.

Remember, Jesus said that we are to seek first the Kingdom of God, and His righteousness. That means we are to seek both the Kingdom and the King. We cannot separate one from the other.

Therefore, the starting place for the firstfruits offering is honoring God and putting Him first when it comes to all your possessions.

Firstfruits is About Increase

Let's look at our key scripture again.

> *Honor the Lord with your possessions,*
> *And with the firstfruits of all your increase;*
> *So your barns will be filled with plenty,*
> *And your vats will overflow with new wine.* — Proverbs 3:9-10 (NKJV)

The firstfruits offering is about *increase*. This is one big difference between firstfruits and the tithe.

We determine our tithe based on our total income. But firstfruits can only apply when our income increases. The firstfruits is a one-time offering of the first portion of an increase over and above what our income was previously.

Let's make up a hypothetical example. In order to keep the numbers simple, let's say that you have $1,000 per month income from your job. If you want to tithe on that amount, you would tithe how much?

$100, because that's 10% of the total.

Now let's say God is blessing the work of your hand just like you see in the promise from Deuteronomy 28:8. You're familiar with that verse, right?

> The Lord will command the blessing on you in your storehouses and in all to which you set your hand, and He will bless you in the land which the Lord your God is giving you. — Deuteronomy 28:8 (NKJV)

There God promises to bless everything you do. Therefore, because of this blessing that God commands on the work of your hand, your boss decides to give you a 5% pay raise. That means your new monthly income is how much? $1,050. It's now $50 more per month than it was previously.

In the first month we receive that pay raise, we can offer a firstfruits offering of $50. In that first month we would still tithe our normal $100, in addition to the firstfruit offering of $50.

We do that just one time, in the first month. That is our firstfruits offering.

Then after that, in the subsequent months we would no longer offer a first fruits offering. Then we would just tithe $105 on the entire $1,050 amount.

Hopefully that makes sense.

We'll talk about more about the practical aspects of what the firstfruits offering looks like here in a bit.

But before we do, let's look at some more scripture.

Cain and Abel

The first formal offering we see in the Bible is in Genesis chapter 4. There we see Cain and Abel, the two sons of Adam and Eve, both come to God with offerings.

We could spend hours discussing why Abel's offering was accepted but Cain's wasn't. Instead I just want to focus on one verse, Genesis 4:4,

> Abel also brought of the firstborn of his flock and of their fat. And the Lord respected Abel and his offering,

Abel brought the firstborn of his flock. He presented his very best to God and God accepted it. This is in line with the firstfruits offering. As new sheep are born into the flock, the flock itself increases. Therefore the firstborn are also the firstfruits of the increase.

The firstfruit offering is something that God also included in the Law. It was a special time of celebration that coincided with harvest time.

However, again I don't want to go into detail of the Law because that's not how we give anyway. We give in faith under grace, not under the obligation or fear of the Law.

Instead, let's go back to our key scripture passage to see the promise available for us to tap into by faith when we choose to offer firstfruits.

The Promise of Firstfruits

> Honor the Lord with your possessions,
> And with the firstfruits of all your increase;
> So your barns will be filled with plenty,
> And your vats will overflow with new wine. — Proverbs 3:9-10 (NKJV)

First, we need to determine if this promise is conditional or unconditional. The obvious answer is that it's conditional on us honoring the Lord with the firstfruits of all our increase.

115

Now I'm not a farmer. I don't have barns or vats. But what I see here is that firstfruits is about seeing my increase blessed.

So the question is, how do we translate this promise into our modern, post-agrarian society?

Well, barns are the places where farmers stored up provision at harvest time to be used throughout the year. Where do we store up our provision today? Typically in our bank accounts.

That means the first fruits offering will help ensure our bank accounts are always filled with plenty of provision.

Wine vats collected the new wine that was pressed out of the grapes. When the vats overflow, that means there is plenty of grapes going into the winepress. I look at the wine vats as representing our means of production, or income.

So that means in addition to having plenty of provision in our bank accounts, God also promises to keep our income flowing to us in response to our first fruits offering.

When you think about it, those promises make sense. Our firstfruits offerings demonstrate that we can be trusted with money because we don't love it. Proverbs says that we are honoring God with our first fruits. Therefore, since we can be trusted to be good stewards over our finances, God can keep income flowing to us knowing it will be handled responsibly.

God supplies seed to those He knows will plant it. Therefore He blesses our increase as a result of our firstfruits offering.

Just like with the tithe, there are all kinds of other ideas about the firstfruits offering out there. I've seen legalistic teaching that says the firstfruits offering is required of believers today.

Nope. That's simply not true.

We can tap into this promise of God by offering the firstfruits of our increase in faith. But there is no requirement for us as New Covenant believers to give firstfruits. None, whatsoever.

I've also seen teaching that says the firstfruits offering must be an annual thing where believers give their entire first month's salary.

Personally I don't see that because the promise of firstfruits there in Proverbs speaks about increase. By interpreting the firstfruits offering as meaning to give the first month's salary in the year, that is effectively making it into some sort of tithe-like offering where we give a twelfth of our annual income instead of giving a tenth with the tithe.

However, the firstfruits offering was never anything like that. We see in Leviticus 23:12-13 that the firstfruits offering consisted of a single male lamb or roughly about a gallon of grain. It's nowhere near a twelfth of the entire harvest.

If, on the other hand, we see our firstfruits as a portion of the increase which Proverbs calls it, then we keep it in the realm of faith.

Increase for Ministries

As we gained understanding in the truths I'm sharing in this book, Lisa and I made the decision to participate in all these forms of giving with our own personal finances. I mentioned in one of the earlier chapters that Lisa and I direct giving by our own nonprofit ministry, NewCREEations. Our board of directors agrees that our ministry participates in all these types of giving as an organization too.

NewCREEations is entirely partner and donor supported. That means we had to pray about what firstfruits offerings might look like for our nonprofit charity.

Here is what we realized. Generally speaking, there are two ways people give to us. They either give a one-time donation, or they start an ongoing monthly partnership.

When someone donates to us, there is no indication of a commitment on their part to continue supporting us financially moving forward.

However, when someone starts a monthly partnership, they are indicating a commitment to continue supporting us. In that case, the income to our ministry has effectively increased by the amount of their partnership moving forward. They certainly aren't under any obligation to support the work God is doing through our ministry month after month, even though they generally do continue to support us.

So what our ministry has agreed to do is whenever someone starts a new partnership with us, we set aside the first month of their new partnership and donate it as a firstfruits offering.

As an example, when someone starts a new partnership for $50 per month, then we give $50 one-time, representing their first month's partnership to another ministry as a firstfruits offering on the increase in our income moving forward that it represents.

Even in our ministry we put God first in the finances. We want our ministry's "barns to be filled with plenty and our vats to be overflowing with new wine." We trust that God is blessing each of those partnerships every single month.

Then in the subsequent months, we add that new partnership to our total income and offer a tithe of the new total.

One result of our approach is that we have remarkably few of our partners who cancel their partnerships. Our ministry partners are incredibly faithful.

At the same time, we also do things like communicate the vision God has given us for the ministry and share examples of the fruit their partnership is producing too. So we're doing what we know to do in the natural as well.

But trust me. We're not *that* good. It is only God and His Spirit that keeps bringing us such faithful partners.

Firstfruits Not Always Applicable

I want to wrap this chapter up by saying that not everyone is in a situation like we are. Because of the way we are applying the firstfruits offering to new monthly partnerships, we give firstfruits offerings quite frequently.

We're blessed with new monthly financial partners for our ministry pretty regularly.

However, for most people that will not necessarily be the case. If you work a traditional job, you might not see a pay raise even once a year. In that case you won't be giving a firstfruits offering very often.

Unless you see an increase in your regular income that will come in on a recurring basis, the firstfruits offering does not apply. You can just set it aside until you see that raise, or that increase in your income.

That's OK. Remember, we give of what we have, not according to what we do not have.

> For if there is first a willing mind, it is accepted according to what one has, and not according to what he does not have. — 2 Corinthians 8:12 (NKJV)

File this information away for when you do see increase in your income.

Also, you can use it to spur on prayer for increase. If you have a desire to give firstfruits, then pray God will direct you to ways to see increase so you can give more.

For whatever reason, I tend to get a lot of questions about the firstfruits offering. Most of them involve scenarios where I don't think firstfruits is really appropriate.

For example, consider someone who has been unemployed for a period of time and then starts a new job. Some might wonder if the firstfruits offering applies to the entire first month's salary. They might want to give everything they earned that first month and then tithe on their income in the subsequent months.

Personally, I think that is not a wise approach in most instances, especially if the person has a bunch of outstanding bills from their time without work. God never intends for us to go into debt in order to give money into the Kingdom.

Remember this. God accepts our offerings based on what we have, not based on what we don't have. Borrowing to give into the Kingdom is very unwise and not in line with God's Kingdom ways.

Instead, I would tithe on the new income and work diligently to pay off any outstanding debt while making sure to get current with any of my bills. God knows how much money you need, even if some of your debt is a result of poor decisions in the past.

Trust God for increase so that you will then have more to give. There is a difference between bread and seed. Don't make the mistake of trying to plant your bread because it won't produce the harvest you need, and it will make you go hungry at the same time.

Let's recap the firstfruits offering.

What is firstfruits? An offering of the first portion of an increase in income.

Who is it given to? To any ministry doing Kingdom work.

Motivation: Generosity, to honor God and put Him first in our finances.

Promise: Barns filled with plenty and vats of wine will overflow, meaning our bank accounts will be filled with plenty of provision and income will keep flowing to us because our means of production will continue to produce over and above what we need.

Key Scripture: Proverbs 3:9-10

> *Honor the Lord with your possessions,*
> *And with the firstfruits of all your increase;*
> *So your barns will be filled with plenty,*
> *And your vats will overflow with new wine.*

Chapter 7

Partnership: Expanding the Kingdom of God

"For who will heed you in this matter? But as his part is who goes down to the battle, so shall his part be who stays by the supplies; they shall share alike."
— 1 Samuel 30:24 (NKJV)

The Power of Partnership

Partnership is a powerful form of giving that is different from the other types in one key respect. Typically each of the other ways of giving in God's Kingdom consist of individual one-time gifts or donations.

However, partnership is a financial commitment to give a regular amount on a consistent basis over a period of time. For example, someone might choose to partner with a ministry for $50 each month.

In the Kingdom of God partnership goes a long way to help ministries and ministers have some consistency in their income for planning purposes. That allows them to go about their assignments with confidence and operate in the blessings of God without having to to constantly rely on miracles from God.

Don't get me wrong. Miracles are indeed amazing and wonderful. But constantly needing to go from miracle to miracle is a stressful way to live. It's no less a walk of faith for ministries to have a consistent foundation of financial partnership in their budget. That gives them the stability of a firm foundation to launch out and take spiritual territory from the enemy.

So it is a very powerful blessing for ministries when we faithfully partner with them financially. At the same time it is also powerful for each of us believers too when we partner with ministries.

To better explain how that works for us, let's look at a story the Bible recounts from the life of David.

A Day in the Life of David

David's life had gotten pretty complicated, and this day was particularly rough. It had been about fifteen years since David made a name for himself by killing Goliath. I'm sure you remember that story.

At first things went pretty well. Saul put David in charge of his entire army. Everything David attempted was successful. The people loved them both. They sang songs about the two of them.

Unfortunately those songs exposed the beginning of trouble between Saul and David. They made David look like more of a hero than Saul. Which made sense if you knew what happened behind the scenes…

Saul could be impulsive, and impatient. And he really worried what other people thought about him, pretty much all the time. On top of that, he was rebellious and stubborn too.

Anyway, long story. But Saul disobeyed a very specific instruction from God to completely destroy the Amalekites. Then he tried to argue with the prophet Samuel about it. So God withdrew His Spirit from Saul.

Which, incidentally was right about the time Samuel secretly anointed

David king to replace Saul. The Bible says, *"the Spirit of the Lord came powerfully upon David from that day forward."* (1 Samuel 16:13)

That move of God's Spirit from Saul to David kind of explains why Saul was so terrified of Goliath. And also why David was able to confront and kill the giant too. Not to mention why David was successful at pretty much everything.

The Bible says that Saul's problem was even worse than God withdrawing His Spirit. After God's Spirit left Saul, a tormenting spirit started harassing Saul from then on. He'd fly into these violent fits of jealous rage, especially when David was around. He'd try to kill David for no good reason except that Saul wanted him dead.

To get rid of his problem he sent David out on the frontier with only a thousand soldiers. I say, "only," because we're talking about less than a half of one percent of the total army Saul had at his disposal.

The hope was that David's small force would be defeated and he'd die. Saul kept giving David these crazy hard assignments, each time thinking David would die in the attempt. Except, instead of getting killed, David kept winning battles...and getting even more famous as a result. Which further enraged Saul.

Saul's jealousy got so bad that he actually spent four years hunting David to try and kill him. David was Saul's public enemy number one!

He truly was a fugitive. Only in David's case the king wanted him dead without cause. David never did anything to justify Saul's hatred of him.

All the while people kept joining David. The Bible says that people who were in distress, debt, or discontent were drawn to David. He became captain over the malcontents and misfits. You could say that David was the lord over the losers, at least to the way things looked to the natural eye.

Later, some of these misfits and apparent losers who were drawn to David during this time eventually became his mighty men. The Bible brags about how truly heroic those guys were in the Kingdom of David.

But that was still a bit off in the future on this difficult day we're talking about.

It got to the point where the fugative group David was leading grew to 600 soldiers. When you added in all their families, David was responsible for a good sized town. It was too many people to hide very well in the wilderness of Israel.

David figured that the best place to hide from a king who is trying to kill him would be in the land of his enemies. So David took his 600 men, and all their families to the city of Gath. That's where Achish, the king of the Philistines lived.

Oh yeah, and Gath was also the home town of Goliath. That giant David had killed nearly fifteen years ago. Can you say, "*Awkward!*"?

Still Loyal to Someone Trying to Kill Him

Needless to say, living in the land of his enemies put David in a bit of a sticky situation. You see, David was a man of honor and integrity. The Bible says he was a man after God's own heart.

So, in spite of the fact that Saul wanted him dead, David was still loyal to the Israelites and even to Saul. By this time David had been presented with two different opportunities to kill Saul and flat out refused to do so.

As far as David was concerned, God was the one who put Saul on the throne of Israel. Even though David himself had secretly been anointed king over Israel by the prophet Samuel years earlier, David refused to be the one to raise a hand against one whom God Himself had installed as king.

David trusted his promotion to come from God, not by his own hand.

So to give himself a little breathing room to live in the land of the Philistines where Saul couldn't get at him, but not be under the Philistine king's nose, David got permission to move with his troops and all their families down to Ziklag, which was a town in the southern part of the land given to Judah back in Joshua's time.

But at this time it was still controlled by the Philistines, even though it was a bit out of the way.

Making a Living Amongst the Enemy

David and his troops had to make a living. Their one skill was fighting, which in that day and time meant they were basically a big raiding party. They earned their living by attacking communities and taking their stuff. And they were good at it.

The fact that David was still loyal to Israel, but was living in Philistine territory with the blessing of the Philistine king put him in a delicate spot. So what David did was attack the allies of the Philistines down further south from where they lived. But he would report back to the Philistine king that he was raiding the Israelites and their allies instead.

To make sure his deception wasn't uncovered, David had a policy of never leaving any survivors when they attacked a place. That way no one could report back who was responsible for the raid.

David could be a brutal guy at times.

For a few years it all worked out OK. Things were trucking along pretty good with this plan. David was chipping away at Israel's enemies. All the while, Achish (the Philistine king) thought David was raiding Israel.

More Complications

Everything was great until just a couple days before this one we're talking about here. That's when Achish told David the Philistines were going to war against Israel. "Oh, and David… you and your men are coming with me on this one."

David's response was simply, "You've seen what I can do."

So even though he *really* didn't want to fight against them, David and his men set out with the Philistine army for war with Israel and Saul.

Did I mention that his life was complicated?

Fortunately for David, the other leaders of the Philistines were able to talk some sense into their king. The short version is that they thought David was very likely a spy and would therefore turn on them in the heat of the battle.

To their way of thinking, David turning on the Philistines while they were fighting the Israelites would be a pretty powerful way for him to get back on Saul's good side. Therefore they forced the king to order David go back home and sit out that particular battle.

First thing the next morning David and his men turned back south for home while the Philistines continued north to war with Saul.

Ziklag Raided

Unfortunately, as soon as the Philistine army headed north to war with Israel, the Amalekites came in and raided some of the southern towns they left unprotected.

Just a side note here. Those were the same Amalekites that God told Saul to wipe off the face of the earth years earlier. Which obviously Saul didn't do, even though he said he did, thereby starting this whole story off in the first place.

The whole thing is all interconnected better than some Hollywood action adventure movie!

When David and his men got back to their home town of Ziklag they found the city burned and all of the people had been taken as slaves. David's family and the families of all his men were gone.

Grief and despair overwhelmed his men and some started talking about killing David for allowing that to happen.

Did I mention he was having a bad day?

Not knowing what to do, David asked God, which is always a good idea anyway. God's response was to go after the raiding party. God said they would catch them and get back everything they lost.

Tired Troops

So they set out after the Amalekites right away. In the course of their pursuit they came to a river.

By this point his men were exhausted. Between all the ground they'd covered, some at a forced march, along with the added emotional toll of finding their homes destroyed and their families taken prisoner, a bunch of his men didn't think they could go on across the river.

Plus it was likely going to be a bit of a hassle to get all their supplies and excess equipment across the river. Getting all their stuff across the river would have slowed them down at a time when every delay reduced the chances of them catching up with the raiders and reuniting with their families.

David made a potentially risky command decision and left a full third of his troops who were just too tired to go any further there on the bank of the river with all their supplies. He continued the pursuit of the Amalekites with the rest of his warriors.

Recovering All

Finally as it was getting dark David and what was left of his army caught up with the raiders and attacked them. The Bible says the battle lasted "from twilight until the evening of the next day."

After traveling hard for at least an entire day, all the emotional trauma of coming home to a burnt out city with their families taken, they end up fighting a 24-hour long battle.

I can't imagine the stress of that. Modern battles are often decided in minutes. The last major battle in Great Britain, the battle of Culloden fought here in Scotland in 1746, was over in less than an hour.

These guys fought an incredibly physically demanding hand-to-hand battle for 24 hours straight. That, even though they had every reason to be exhausted before this excruciatingly long fight even began.

But in the end they got everything and everyone back, apparently without losing a man themselves.

Actually the spoils of victory were even bigger than expected. The Amalekites had raided many more places than just their town, Ziklag. So David's men really ended up getting all their stuff back plus a whole lot more.

Once they gathered up everything they headed back to Ziklag.

Conflict in the Ranks

When they got back to the third of the army that were too tired to cross the river and fight, some of the troops who fought in the battle started to grumble.

Let's pick up the story in 1 Samuel chapter 30, verse 21,

> *Now David came to the two hundred men who had been so weary that they could not follow David, whom they also had made to stay at the Brook Besor. So they went out to meet David and to meet the people who were with him. And when David came near the people, he greeted them. Then all the wicked and worthless men of those who went with David answered and said, "Because they did not go with us, we will not give them any of the spoil that we have recovered, except for every man's wife and children, that they may lead them away and depart."*
>
> *But David said, "My brethren, you shall not do so with what the Lord has given us, who has preserved us and delivered into our hand the troop that came against us. For who will heed you in this matter? But as his part is who goes down to the battle, so shall his part be who stays by the supplies; they shall share alike." So it was, from that day forward; he made it a statute and an ordinance for Israel to this day.* — 1 Samuel 30:21-25 (NKJV)

Equal Rewards

Basically some of the guys who fought in the battle thought that the ones who were too tired to continue on didn't deserve any share of the loot they took from the Amalekites. Their attitude seems to make sense: You fight the fight, you get the loot.

Yet look how the Bible describes the men who expressed this view. The Bible says they were "wicked and worthless men."

Keep in mind these are some of the same men who marched for God knows how long in pursuit of their enemy and then fought with them more then 24 hours straight to completely win the day.

Oh, and in the process of all this, they were doing a task that God originally told Saul to deal with years earlier.

Their actions were good. But their hearts were completely wrong.

At the same time it might be understandable to think that those 200 guys who were too tired to go and fight were maybe a little on the lazy side. After all we're talking about a fight that lasted an entire night and all the next day. While that was happening the 200 were hanging out resting at the oasis with all the supplies.

The Bible says that river is called the Brook Besor. It flows west through lower Israel out to the Mediterranean. It forms a lush oasis in the middle of some dry country. That would make it a very appealing place to get distracted from the task at hand.

If we're talking about who earned what, it seems obvious that those who actually fought the battle were more deserving than those who stayed back with the stuff. But David, a man after God's own heart, said that's not the case.

In fact, David pointed out that their victory was given to them by God and not due to their own military prowess. He basically said those guys were talking crazy talk. No one should listen to what they were saying.

Then he makes it simple for everyone to understand,

> *The share of the man who stayed with the supplies is to be the same as that of him who went down to the battle. All will share alike. — 1 Samuel 30:24b (NIV)*

Everyone who participates at any level gets the same reward. Period.

Ultimately that decision was so powerful that the same policy carried over into the Kingdom of Israel after David became king.

Keep in mind that the Kingdom of David is a type and shadow of the Kingdom of God. Therefore we can look at the way things worked in David's kingdom to get an idea how they work in the Kingdom of God.

That is the promise of partnership today — equal reward.

How Partnership Works Today

That's a long winded way to show you how the Kingdom of God operates today in the area of financial partnership.

In the Kingdom of God, partnership is serious business. Because, just like how David could not conquer the Amalekites without men to stay behind with the supplies, or as the King James Version says, "tarrieth by the stuff;" ministry today cannot happen without financial partnership.

And just like then, today those who finance ministry get an equal share with those who go and do the work. They get the exact same rewards as the missionaries they are financially supporting.

For example, look at what Jesus said in Mark 10:29-30,

> *So Jesus answered and said, "Assuredly, I say to you, there is no one who has left house or brothers or sisters or father or mother or wife or children or lands, for My sake and the gospel's, who shall not receive a hundredfold now in this time—houses and brothers and sisters and mothers and children and lands, with persecutions—and in the age to come, eternal life. — Mark 10:29-30 (NKJV)*

That right there is God's promise for missionaries. Not everyone can leave everything behind and head out on the mission field. Partnership is the mechanism that allows people who cannot go out to the mission field to receive an equal share in the reward — now, in this time — as those who do go.

The reality is, no person accomplishes a work single handed. Even Jesus needed staff! God's plan on this earth is to do work through and with people.

If I'm completely transparent, Lisa and I could not be here in Scotland without the financial support of our ministry partners. Without them, the Bible college campus we head up would not be happening today and therefore it is unlikely that the lives of our students would be transformed in the manner and to the degree that they have since we opened our doors.

The transformation that's happening in their lives today as students in the Bible college campus we head up is a direct result of all the people who have partnered financially with what God is doing here in Scotland through our ministry.

That's how partnership works for those that Jesus talked about who are sent.

Expanding the Kingdom

The purpose of partnership is to expand the Kingdom of God. The guys that stayed back with the stuff gave David and the rest of their warriors a secure jumping off point to go to battle. Staying with the stuff and guarding their supply lines allowed them the security they needed to focus on the primary task at hand — defeating their enemy and reclaiming what was rightfully theirs.

Keep in mind that David made it a point to inquire of the Lord what he should do before he headed out to battle that day. As a result his assignment came directly from the Lord.

In the same way, financial partnership allows ministers and ministries to carry out their God-given assignments too. These assignments all have one overarching purpose — to expand the Kingdom of God.

That's the purpose of partnership — expanding the Kingdom of God.

Partnership expands God's Kingdom because it amplifies the effectiveness of ministers by supplying more resources, enabling them to reach more people and impact more lives.

For example, we couldn't reach the online audience we do, teach the students at our Bible college campus here in Scotland, or travel to the places we go without the faithful financial support of our ministry partners. That's hundreds of thousands of lives who are being touched by the Kingdom of God to varying degrees each year because of the multiplying effect of partnership.

Some of those lives touched may only get a quick glance at an article on our website, while others are being discipled in depth over two or three years. The Kingdom of God is being expanded by degrees through every single life touched by our organization.

And we're just one organization out of who knows how many ministries around the world who are doing good work expanding God's Kingdom, all with the help of untold millions of ministry partners.

Increase by Association

Partnership means increase by association. It's a simple fact of life that we become like those we associate and surround ourselves with.

We see the negative example of this in 1 Corinthians 15:33,

> Do not be deceived: "Evil company corrupts good habits."

I've seen secular studies claim that we become the average of the five people we spend the most time with. If that's the case, and we make three of those folks the Father, Son, and Holy Spirit, that's going to affect our average in a very positive way!

I think about things like that.

This increase by association is true when it comes to anointing. Partnering with ministers and ministries brings you under the anointing God has given them. In fact, the more closely you associate with an anointed ministry, the more your own anointing in that area can also increase.

We see a supernatural example of that with the anointing Elisha received because of his association with Elijah — 2 Kings 2:6-14,

> Then Elijah said to him, "Stay here, please, for the Lord has sent me on to the Jordan."
>
> But he said, "As the Lord lives, and as your soul lives, I will not leave you!" So the two of them went on. And fifty men of the sons of the prophets went and stood facing them at a distance, while the two of them stood by the Jordan. Now Elijah took his mantle, rolled it up, and struck the water; and it was divided this way and that, so that the two of them crossed over on dry ground.
>
> And so it was, when they had crossed over, that Elijah said to Elisha, "Ask! What may I do for you, before I am taken away from you?"
>
> Elisha said, "Please let a double portion of your spirit be upon me."
>
> So he said, "You have asked a hard thing. Nevertheless, if you see me when I am taken from you, it shall be so for you; but if not, it shall not be so." Then it happened, as they continued on and talked, that suddenly a chariot of fire appeared with horses of fire, and separated the two of them; and Elijah went up by a whirlwind into heaven.
>
> And Elisha saw it, and he cried out, "My father, my father, the chariot of Israel and its horsemen!" So he saw him no more. And he took hold of his own clothes and tore them into two pieces. He also took up the mantle of Elijah that had fallen from him, and went back and stood by the bank of the Jordan. Then he took the mantle of Elijah that had fallen from him, and struck the water, and said, "Where is the Lord God of Elijah?" And when he also had struck the water, it was divided this way and that; and Elisha crossed over.

Elisha's very first miracle was exactly the same as Elijah's very last miracle. He started at the exact point his mentor left off.

We also know that Elisha did, in fact, receive a double portion of the spirit that was on Elijah. In the Bible, Elisha is recorded as having done twice as many miracles as his mentor did.

God's anointing on a minister or ministry flows over onto those who partner with it financially.

This increase by association also works in the financial/business realm too.

We see this with Jacob and Laban.

> And Laban said to him, "Please stay, if I have found favor in your eyes, for I have learned by experience that the Lord has blessed me for your sake." — Genesis 30:27 (NKJV)

Laban recognized that his own business was blessed and he personally prospered because of the anointing and blessing of God on Jacob's life.

We also see this same thing happen in the life of Joseph. Potiphar knew that his personal holdings were blessed because of the anointing of God on Joseph's life.

> The Lord was with Joseph, and he was a successful man; and he was in the house of his master the Egyptian. And his master saw that the Lord was with him and that the Lord made all he did to prosper in his hand. So Joseph found favor in his sight, and served him. Then he made him overseer of his house, and all that he had he put under his authority. So it was, from the time that he had made him overseer of his house and all that he had, that the Lord blessed the Egyptian's house for Joseph's sake; and the blessing of the Lord was on all that he had in the house and in the field. Thus he left all that he had in Joseph's hand, and he did not know what he had except for the bread which he ate. — Genesis 39:2-6 (NKJV)

As long as Joseph was running Potiphar's business, the only thing Potiphar had to think about was the food he put in his own mouth. The anointing and blessing that was on Joseph caused Potiphar's business interests to thrive.

I've seen the same thing work in my own life too. At one point I had a revenue sharing arrangement with an employer. While that arrangement was in place the sales for that part of the business covered by our arrangement grew steadily.

Unfortunately I fell behind in holding up my end of the arrangement and the employer decided to end the arrangement. It was a totally understandable business decision on their part because I did drop the ball. I certainly never disputed their decision to end their profit sharing with me.

However, I still had access to the sales figures for that part of the business. So I could see that the sales for that department plateaued right when the profit sharing was stopped. I doubt they would have made the connection. But the timing was clear. God was blessing that part of the business for our sake as a way to get more income to me and Lisa. But as soon as that connection was cut, God no longer had a reason to go out of His way to bless that part of the business.

We carry the favor and anointing of God wherever we go, just like Jacob and Joseph did, as do the ministers and ministries we choose to partner with.

That means we can share in the financial anointing of those we partner with too.

Sow Where You Want to Go

I'm sure you've heard that saying before, "sow where you want to go." Sometimes we can get so familiar with a phrase that it becomes cliché in our minds.

But this one is true. There is genuine power in partnering with a ministry that is ahead of you or is already seeing success in an area you are looking to step into.

For an example of this in scripture, let's look at Elijah and the widow at Zarephath:

> And Elijah said to her, "Do not fear; go and do as you have said, but make me a small cake from it first, and bring it to me; and afterward make some for yourself and your son. For thus says the Lord God of

> Israel: *'The bin of flour shall not be used up, nor shall the jar of oil run dry, until the day the Lord sends rain on the earth.' "* — 1 Kings 17:13-14 (NKJV)

The widow sowed into Elijah's ministry by giving him the first portion of what little she had left. This act of faith on her part moved her food supply out of the world's cursed system and into the Kingdom of God, allowing it to be blessed and multiplied.

The result was she had enough to eat and stayed alive until the famine ended.

"Sow where you want to go" also applies to us today. Lisa and I have seen it work in our own lives.

As we were first thinking about coming to Bible college in our early days of watching the founder of the school we went to on TV, we saw a short promotion for an organization in his ministry that is responsible for planting their Bible college campuses around the world.

Something stirred in both of our hearts and we thought, "We want to sow into that!"

We started a monthly partnership with that part of his organization way back then. That was years before God said anything to ether of us about Scotland or about being a part of the his organization. It was even before we were enrolled as students ourselves!

We were personally sowing into our own future — we were sowing where were were ultimately going — even though we didn't realize it at the time! And we still partner financially with that part of his organization personally, even today. I mean, why wouldn't we partner with an organization that is so near and dear to our own heart?

We also partner with several other ministries and organizations around the world, all for various reasons.

One of the longest running partnerships we have is with a ministry that we don't even really line up with theologically anymore. However God hasn't released us from that partnership.

In fact, what God told us is that we are sowing faithfulness by continuing our partnership with that organization even though it doesn't seem to make sense. I know our firstfruits offerings have a big part to play in the faithfulness of the partners with our own ministry.

At the same time, by sowing faithfulness into that other ministry we are harvesting faithfulness in our own ministry too.

Partnership is powerful.

Let's review.

What is partnership? Money given to help a ministry (or minister) accomplish its mission.

Who is it given to? To any ministry (or minister) taking territory from the enemy for the Kingdom of God.

Motivation: Expand the Kingdom of God.

Promise: All who participate in the battle in any capacity get an equal share of the reward. It doesn't matter if they are on the front lines or hanging back with the supplies all will share alike in the plunder.

Key Scripture: 1 Samuel 30:24

> *For who will heed you in this matter? But as his part is who goes down to the battle, so shall his part be who stays by the supplies; they shall share alike.*

Chapter 8

How to Plant and Receive a Harvest

"But other seed fell on good ground and yielded a crop that sprang up,
increased and produced: some thirtyfold, some sixty, and some a hundred."
— Mark 4:8 (NKJV)

Quick Review

In this chapter we will look at the part of Kingdom finance that I find most exciting. Actually I think most people find this part exciting, which is why so many ministers start here.

Sowing and reaping is where we can see some amazing things happen. But before we get started, let's think about the other types of giving we've covered so far.

With giving alms, God promises to repay. Thats a one-for-one return on what we give. The purpose of alms giving is to care for the poor and alleviate suffering. We are motivated to give alms out of compassion for others. Alms can be in any amount given to anyone, regardless of whether the recipients are believers or not. And we saw that alms is the one type of giving that Jesus instructed us to never talk about because God loves people and He wants us to guard their dignity.

The tithe is the foundation of our Kingdom financial prosperity plan. It involves giving a tenth (10%) of our income to Jesus, usually into our local church. The purpose of the tithe is to fund the ministry work of our local churches. Our motivation to tithe is simple obedience to put God first in our finances and to meet the condition so we can receive the promise. That promise is the real power of the tithe, because God promises to rebuke the devourer on our behalf. At the same time, tithing moves our finances out of the earth's cursed mammon system and into the Kingdom of God because of the Law of Firstfruits.

Where the tithe protects our finances from loss, the firstfruits offering blesses any increase that God brings to us. The purpose of firstfruits offerings is to be an extra blessing to Kingdom organizations. We are motivated by generosity to put God first in our finances and give our firstfruits into the Kingdom. By putting Him first we demonstrate in faith that God is our source and not the money. We give God the legal right to keep our storehouse full and our means of production flowing abundantly.

Partnership helps expand the Kingdom of God. It is that desire to see God's Kingdom expand that is the primary motivation for us to partner financially with ministries. By partnering with ministries with our giving consistently over time, we help with their financial stability so they can focus on the work God called them to without the stress of believing for miracle after miracle in their provision. At the same time partnership enables us to share in the rewards of the minister or ministry we are partnering with. That way we can have an equal share of the anointing of the ministries we partner with.

All of those different types of giving tap into powerful promises in God's word. They each accomplish different things for the Kingdom of God to benefit others, while at the same time helping our own finances in very different and specific ways.

But when we get to sowing and reaping, things can get pretty amazing. In the world of business, a return on your investment of 5-10% is generally considered pretty good. Yet that seems pretty lame compared to the promise for sowing into the Kingdom of God of thirty, sixty, or a hundredfold harvest. Which one sounds better to you?

However, that only happens when our giving is mixed with faith. That means we must understand the truth God says about it. And if we don't establish the rest of the things we've already covered in this book first, it is easy to get way out of balance when it comes to planting and harvesting, or sowing and reaping in our finances.

We need to understand that there's a huge difference between the ways things work in the Kingdom of God versus how they work in the world.

Seed vs. Bread

There's one thing I want to emphasize before we get into talking about planting and harvesting. We already mentioned it briefly. But I want to make sure we highlight the importance of differentiating between our seed and our bread.

2 Corinthians 9:10 says that God supplies seed for the sower and bread for food.

Let me ask you a question. What will happen if you bury a loaf of bread in the ground? Will anything sprout up and grow from that loaf of bread?

No. Of course not. The bread will just decay and rot there in the dirt. If you try to plant your bread, it won't produce anything of value. You certainly won't receive a harvest. And if you make planting all your bread a habit, you may very well end up starving.

Unfortunately this error is more common than it really should be. Some folks will hear some teaching about sowing and reaping, perhaps along with a particularly powerful testimony of someone who sowed their last bit of provision, then saw God came through in a big way so they received a big harvest.

Then they'll take that teaching and that testimony, treat it like a formula, and just give everything away without ever really checking in with God about any of their giving.

I'm here to tell you it doesn't work that way. Planting your bread will not produce a harvest. Doing so moves you out of the arena of God's blessing and puts you squarely in the land of crisis. And when you linger in the land of crisis, you will end up drifting from miracle to miracle just to survive.

Granted, living from miracle to miracle is an exciting place to be. But it sure is stressful, and unnecessarily so.

Anytime you fall into survival mode, then you are doing good just to have enough to make it. You aren't thriving, and you certainly are not able to be much of a blessing to others.

At the same time it is also possible to fall into the ditch on the other side of the road and eat your seed. Honestly, this is what the overwhelming majority of believers do today. Because you can eat your seed and still at least get some nutrition from it.

However, the more of your seed that you eat today, the less you have available to put in the ground when it comes time to plant. And that reduces the size of the harvest you will ultimately receive.

In most cases, one big reason why believers don't prosper is because they are eating all their seed in addition to eating their bread. Therefore they never realize that they have seed to plant and don't ever participate in real sowing into God's Kingdom.

In many cases, even when believers are giving, it may very well be that they think they are sowing when they are not. Often what happens is they participate in one of the other types of giving, such as alms or the tithe. They give their alms expecting a thirty, sixty, or hundredfold return, never realizing that the promise for alms is simple replacement.

Knowing the difference between what should be seed for us to sow and what is bread for us to eat also helps keep our hearts pure and undefiled by the love of money. When you are looking for opportunities to give to others, you aren't looking for ways to feed your own flesh with greed.

All that to say, it's critical to know the difference between your seed and your bread. But here's the hard part. There is no formula which tells those two apart.

The ability to differentiate between the two flows from a healthy relationship with God. He is the only one who can tell you for sure what is your bread, good to eat, and what is best to set aside for your seed.

Your relationship with God is critical because what is bread for me, might be seed for you, and vice versa.

That's the danger of trying to simply copy the actions someone else takes in their giving outside of the intimacy of our relationship with Jesus. I might follow exactly what you do, down to the last penny, and still have it totally wrong even though when you do it, it's exactly right.

The act of someone else giving away everything they have might be a powerful step of faith as they sow just the right amount of seed to reap a massive harvest. Yet, at the same time, doing that same exact thing might for me be a completely faithless act as I try and force God to bail me out from my own stupidity because I've just buried all my bread in the ground.

Remember, it is the Holy Spirit who guides us. And He will do so in a way that glorifies Jesus, not some system or formula. It is vital that we conduct all of our giving in harmony with our relationship with God.

Otherwise you will see very inconsistent results.

Even though there is no formula, I can offer you some guidance on how to know the difference between your seed and your bread. I believe the key here is to follow peace.

As you step into this, you will learn to discern God's voice in this arena. Then you will just know what you should do in the situation because you will have peace about it.

That doesn't mean what God tells you to give will always be comfortable. Let me bring your attention to this verse in Psalms.

Those who sow in tears
Shall reap in joy. — Psalms 126:5 (NKJV)

There will likely be times when God asks you to give an amount that genuinely feels painful. And it's quite possible that giving that much will make absolutely no sense whatsoever in the natural.

The key is that you will still have peace about what you are giving despite however your flesh may be reacting.

And if you're married, it is best to have unity with your spouse with your giving. I know I've gone ahead and done some things even though Lisa wasn't really in agreement. I've yet to see that ever work out well for us.

For example, we had some giving in place recently that I really needed to adjust. I pushed out ahead of Lisa and started a partnership with a specific goal in mind because I felt like I needed to "make" something happen.

That's a mistake on my part.

In that case, I think where I missed it is on the timing. Historically, that's the part which can be the biggest challenge for me to get right. I'll often hear the what and the where. But then I have a tendency to assume on the when. Typically I assume the when is "now" but God is really meaning for me to get ready for His when, which is coming up.

Fortunately, one of the best indicators of the right timing for me, especially with financial matters, is when Lisa and I are both in agreement about the thing.

Because I'm the visionary in our marriage, I have a tendency to push out ahead of where she is with God in some areas.

When I do that, I'm missing God's timing. Yet I can look back through our lives and see those times when our hearts came into agreement with one another and see how perfect the timing was for that decision or action.

Notice I said our hearts come into agreement with one another. It's not a case of her always coming into agreement with me. I can be a bit of a bulldozer at times. And there have been times in our lives when Lisa has gone along to get along. Trust me, that is very different than having our hearts truly aligned about something.

In this particular instance I'm thinking about, that's pretty much exactly what happened. Which means it was kind of dumb...on my part.

It's so much better for us to both wait until we are in unity, especially when we are praying about plating large amounts of seed. The results we see then are often quite amazing.

If your spouse is not a believer, or is completely not on the same page as you when it comes to giving, I want to reassure you, that's OK. You're just in a different situation than Lisa and I are in.

Remember this. God knows where you are. And he knows what you can and cannot do while still loving and respecting your spouse. God will not ask you to do something, to give something, that is beyond the boundaries of the authority you have in your marriage.

Remember, it's not about total amounts. The Kingdom of God is more about percentages anyway. So please don't feel pressure to give in ways that your husband or wife is dead set against.

Give in the ways you are able to, no matter how small. Watch God bless that giving. And then allow those testimonies to speak to your spouse's heart. I suspect you'll find that they become more and more open to your desire to give when they see how God blesses what you do.

Be patient. Allow the Holy Spirit time and room to work in your spouse's heart.

SOWING AND REAPING AND MONEY

If you remember back in chapter four, we introduced the law of planting and harvesting, also called the law of sowing and reaping. As a reminder, here's that passage in the Bible.

Do not be deceived, God is not mocked; for whatever a man sows, that he will also reap. For he who sows to his flesh will of the flesh reap corruption, but he who sows to the Spirit will of the Spirit reap everlasting life. — Galatians 6:7-8 (NKJV)

We said this law of planting and harvesting is universal. It applies to both the natural world and to the spiritual realm too. God hardwired it into the universe at creation, just like He hardwired the law of gravity.

We said the law of sowing and reaping means you harvest the same exact thing you plant. Like begets like and a seed only produces after its own kind. We will only harvest the same thing we plant.

However, it turns out money is a special case here when it comes to the law of planting and harvesting. We can actually plant money and harvest something totally different than the cash that we sowed into the Kingdom of God.

How does that work?

I mean if seeds only reproduce in kind, how is it we can sow money and receive a harvest of something else entirely?

Well here's the thing about money. Currency is simply a medium of exchange. Remember, money is entirely a worldly man-made creation developed to facilitate commerce.

The truth is, money in and of itself doesn't do much for me. I can't eat currency. Money won't transport me from here to there. Cash won't keep me warm and dry at night.

Money by itself is pretty useless to me. It has almost no intrinsic value whatsoever.

Instead, the real value of money lies in all the different things I can turn that money into. With money, I can buy food, put fuel in my car, and rent a wonderfully cozy home. When I exchange money for those things by paying for them, I am naming my money something of real value to me.

Every single day I name part of my money something that I don't yet have. Every month I call some of my money "groceries". Some of it gets called "house". Every month we call some of our money "high speed internet," "mobile phones," "electricity," "gas", and "insurance."

We name our money other stuff all the time within the mammon system. And it turns out, we're going to see here in a little bit how we can do exactly the same thing with money in the Kingdom of God.

Key Scripture

With all that said, let's look at our key verse for this chapter.

> *But other seed fell on good ground and yielded a crop that sprang up, increased and produced: some thirtyfold, some sixty, and some a hundred.* — Mark 4:8 (NKJV)

Obviously this is the promise from the parable of the sower. Jesus makes it very clear what He means by that parable. The parable of the sower is one of the few parables where the Bible records Jesus explaining the meaning explicitly.

In verse 14 of that same chapter Jesus says, *"The sower sows the word."*

Therefore the "seed" in this parable represents the word of God. It is God's word that is sown and produces the harvest.

Sometimes folks will object to the thirty, sixty, hundred fold return being applied to money because Jesus says the seed is the word. And I get where they are coming from.

In truth, I'm glad Jesus did not say the sower sows money. Because if he did, then it would *only* apply to money.

Fortunately, because Jesus said the seed is the word, that means this promise of thirty, sixty, hundredfold return applies to *everything* found in scripture. We can take any principle or promise that we see in scripture, sow it into our lives, or into the world around us, and see this thirty, sixty, hundredfold return.

Therefore, because there are so many scriptures that deal explicitly with money and finances, that means this promise applies to those too, along with everything else we see in the Bible. Any time the word of God finds fertile ground in a receptive heart it will produce a bountiful harvest.

This includes passages within the word that deal with money and finances.

It just so happens that money is tangible, and quantifiable. That means we can objectively measure results. The enemy doesn't like that!

Remember chapter three where we talked bout God being glorified when He answers our prayers? We pointed out that the more specific our prayers are, the more glory He gets when He answers them.

The same thing happens when we start inviting God to get involved with our finances. When we can start correlating what we do with our money with the things God is doing on our behalf, things can get pretty exciting!

And God gets glory in the process. The enemy *really* doesn't like that!

Remember our story about our car situation? Remember how God replaced our old car with a much newer and much nicer car? And He did that for us despite the fact that I was stupid and drove our car down a tractor path between two fields that I had no business being on in that kind of vehicle.

God not only protected our finances from the devourer trying to use my stupidity to drain off our finances in a big way, He also opened the floodgates of Heaven and poured out a blessing, of what happens to be the nicest car I've ever owned.

And He did that because of the promise He made in his word about the tithe, which Lisa and I chose to claim by faith after we met the condition associated with that promise by tithing.

Let me ask you this. Who gets the glory in that whole car situation?

God does!

There's no way I could have worked it so that an insurance company would track us down 28 years after I opened our account with them, at exactly the moment when we needed that money. That whole deal has God's fingerprints all over it.

We get blessed, sure. But He gets all the glory.

And you know what? We are able to bless others from the overflow of that blessing. That car allows us to provide comfortable transportation for others as we minister here in Scotland.

For example, when we have guest speakers come into the Bible college, we can drive up to Glasgow to the airport and bring them back down to Dumfries without any hassle.

We are all generally able to be more "in the moment" and fresh when we arrive because we were blessed with a comfortable vehicle to get there in. It's a little thing, I know. But that's an example of how that blessing God gave Chris and Lisa overflows and blesses others too.

What is a Hundredfold Return?

There are a few different ways to look at the hundredfold return. If we take what this says literally in the original Greek, it means "one hundred times as much."

And I see a lot of people who treat sowing and reaping that way. Typically that type of thinking goes like this. I have fifty dollars to put into the offering. I'm believing for a hundredfold return. Therefore I'm expecting to receive a harvest of $5,000 on this seed.

Sometimes that might be the case. But I think we'll see here in a bit why that's probably not the best interpretation of the hundredfold return.

Then I've heard other people fixate on that English word and say that hundredfold means fold it one hundred times. That interpretation is like taking a piece of paper and folding it in half. Then fold it in half again, and so on until you've folded it 100 times.

They get excited about that because the numbers get crazy huge when you do that.

For example, take a piece of letter sized, or A4 printer paper and try to fold it in half as many different times as you can. After folding it only 6 times you will have have 64 rectangles. (Six times is the most I've been able to fold a piece of paper that size when I do this example for our students.)

The thing is the thickness doubles with every fold. If you were to do the math, how many folds of this piece of paper do you think it would take to reach to the moon? The answer is a surprisingly small 45 times.

And that would give you about 35.2 trillion rectangles.

One hundred folds approaches the width of the known universe. Seriously. It gets that thick. And how many rectangles does it produce?

1,267,650,600,228,229,401,496,703,205,376

1 Nonillion, 267 Octillion, 650 Septillion, 600 Sextillion, 228 Quintillion, 229 Quadrillion , 401 Trillion, 496 Billion, 703 Million, 205 Thousand, 376, give or take. I looked it up. That's a 1 with 30 other numbers behind it.

Somehow I don't think that's what Jesus meant when He mentioned a hundredfold harvest.

For one thing, if you noticed, all the squares are just smaller portions of the same whole original piece of paper. We aren't gaining any more paper by folding the same thing over and over. There is still just the same single piece of paper we started with.

Therefore, as fun as those numbers are to think about, it really doesn't make much sense to say that's what Jesus meant.

Instead, I personally think the best way to understand what Jesus meant by the hundredfold return is that we see the maximum possible potential for that seed.

Take an apple seed as an example. What is the full potential of that apple seed?

Is it a single tree that produces hundreds of apples every year?

But what if seeds from those apples were also planted? Then perhaps that one seed could eventually be responsible for producing an entire orchard of apple trees all producing tons of fruit each and every year.

Or maybe that one seed has the potential to ultimately, down the road, produce hundreds of apple orchards all over the world.

What is the maximum potential of that original seed? Really it depends on the faith and vision of the one who plants that seed, doesn't it.

Let that thought sink in for a moment.

Our Capacity to Receive

One way to measure how much faith we have is by how much capacity we have to collect the harvest we are believing for. God will never give us more than our capacity can handle. God loves us, so He will not destroy us by overloading us with increase and overwhelming us.

We see this over and over in scripture.

For example, when the widow went to Elisha about the debt she owed, Elisha asked what she had in her house. The only thing she had was a little bit of oil. So Elisha told her to get as many jars as she could and pour the oil into all of them, which she did.

Then the Bible says this,

> When the containers were full, she said to her son, "Bring me another container."
>
> He said to her, "There isn't another container." Then the oil stopped flowing. — 2 Kings 4:6 (WEB)

The woman's faith was measured by the number of containers she gathered to pour the oil into. The miracle stopped when all of those containers were full and the oil reached her capacity to receive it.

We see a New Testament example of this in Luke. There we see something interesting happen after Peter allowed Jesus to use one of his boats during His ministry time,

> When He had stopped speaking, He said to Simon, "Launch out into the deep and let down your nets for a catch."
>
> But Simon answered and said to Him, "Master, we have toiled all night and caught nothing; nevertheless at Your word I will let down the net." And when they had done this, they caught a great number of fish, and their net was breaking. So they signaled to their partners in the other boat to come and help them. And they came and filled both the boats, so that they began to sink. — Luke 5:4-7 (NKJV)

There is much we can learn from that passage. But notice how much fish Peter and his business partners caught here. The catch was just as much as his nets and boats could handle. The nets were at the breaking point, though they didn't break. And the boats were at the point of sinking, though they didn't sink.

I believe this is what the hundredfold harvest truly looks like. Peter sowed the use of his boat into the ministry of Jesus by allowing Him to use it as a platform for teaching so Jesus could reach more people. In return Peter received a harvest of exactly as much income as his business was equipped to handle.

And here's a side note. Notice that Peter's partners were blessed too and shared in the harvest even without exercising any faith themselves. The harvest came in response to Peter's faith. We see this when he said he would let down the nets one more time purely in response to the word of Jesus. Peter's faith brought the harvest and his partners also benefitted. This is an excellent picture of how we share in the blessing when we partner with ministries too.

Our capacity to handle increase is a significant factor that can limit the maximum potential of the harvest we receive from God. So we need to consider our capacity when determining how much we are setting our faith to receive. Trying to believe for vastly more than we have the capacity to receive is unwise because it sets our heart up to see our hope disappointed, which is harmful to us.

This means we will do well to seek the Holy Spirit to show us what our capacity truly is. When God is looking to grow us beyond our current capacity, He will also give us a plan on how to expand our capacity.

As a practical example, Lisa and I would be unwise to set our faith to believe God for, say, ten million dollars of income into our ministry organization in the next year as I write this even though we have the theoretical ability to receive that much. And while a single donor could theoretically write a check for the whole amount, the reality is that that kind of income generally comes from a great many partners all giving much smaller amounts.

The hard truth is that we don't yet have the administrative systems in place to handle that many partners. There is a real cost involved for staff, systems, and infrastructure to support growth. We must grow our capacity to receive just as we also must grow our faith to receive.

So know there will always be tension between stretching our faith to receive more from God, and the limits our capacity to handle increase put on God's ability to bless us.

The good news is that the Holy Spirit can reveal plans for us to increase our capacity. There are any number of ways God can show us how to grow our capacity to receive. He might show us to hire more staff, or purchase a piece of equipment or software that will make us more efficient.

Perhaps in your case the Holy Spirit might guide you to add a new revenue stream to your business, or start a new business entirely. Or God might have something else entirely different in mind, custom tailored for you and your situation.

Remember what we said back in the first chapter, God supplies supernaturally through natural means. If you find yourself having trouble receiving increase, it may be that you just need to expand your capacity to receive.

How Farmers Plant

When we start talking about sowing and reaping, it is helpful to think about how a farmer plants. What you'll soon come to understand is that most people do things backwards when they sow financial seeds.

Here's how most believers approach sowing. It's the offering time and the first thing they do is look to their wallet to see how much seed they have to give. Then whatever that amount is, they will declare they are receiving a hundred times that amount back as their hundredfold return.

They might have $20 in their wallet to give in an offering. So they decide that's a seed and they think they will then receive $2,000 back as their harvest on that seed.

Unfortunately very few people ever see where that seed produces that particular harvest, at least not in any way we can correlate a connection.

As a result, a great many people give up on giving. Hope deferred makes the heart sick. So they conclude that promise Jesus made must not include anything with our finances.

However, the problem isn't with the law of sowing and reaping. The problem is with a misunderstanding of how planting and harvesting works. We can look at how farmers plant to get some insight on this.

Instead of starting with how much seed they have available, a farmer starts with the size harvest he is looking for. If a farmer wants to harvest 100 tons of corn, he knows he cannot just plant two corn seeds.

Even at their best, two corn plants cannot produce 100 tons of corn, at least not in one harvest.

Instead, the farmer decides what size harvest he is looking to bring in. Then he looks at how much seed he must sow in order to reap that size harvest. And he also looks at which field he will plant it in.

The farmer starts with the harvest in mind then plants however much seed he needs to produce that size harvest.

And this lines up with something Jesus said about giving too.

> *Give, and it will be given to you: good measure, pressed down, shaken together, and running over will be put into your bosom. For with the same measure that you use, it will be measured back to you.*
> — Luke 6:38 (NKJV)

Jesus said that your harvest is determined by the *measure* of the seed you use. That means most people are doing it backwards.

Instead of saying, "I've got some seed here. How much can I get for this?" we should start with the end in mind and work it backwards.

No farmer is going to fling his seed willy nilly wherever and hope to get a harvest. Well, no successful farmer will anyway. Instead the successful farmer is deliberate and intentional about the seed he sows.

We should be just like that successful farmer and start with the harvest we are looking for. We take that harvest to God and ask Him to show us how much seed to sow, and what field to sow it into so that we can receive that harvest which we are believing to receive.

Who better to align the measure of our giving with the harvest we are looking to receive than the one who knows the end from the beginning?

We can get with God and find out from Him how much seed we need to sow and what field to plant it in, to get the harvest we are believing for.

Think about it. Proverbs 16:9 says this:

> *A man's heart plans his way,*
> *But the Lord directs his steps.*

According to that scripture, when we plan we give God something to work with. We step out in faith first, *then* He will guide our steps. The key is looking to Him throughout the process.

This works with sowing and reaping. Lisa and I have seen it in our lives over and over again.

Why This is Not a Formula

Sometimes you hear folks call those who teach on how to prosper in the Kingdom of God as "name it and claim it" preachers. Less charitable folks might say, "blab it and grab it."

I'll be honest with you, I avoided prosperity teaching altogether because so much of it comes across as formulaic. If you give "x" then you will receive "y".

Some teaching I've heard that talks about "naming your seed" seems like attempts to manipulate or control God, to force Him to do what we want Him to do.

It just never sat right with me.

But that is not at all what I'm talking about here.

You see none of this works at all outside of our relationship with God. He's the one who sets the measure of our seed. He tells us what field to plant in to receive the harvest we are looking for. Then He's the one who provides the increase for us to harvest.

If we try to do this without His insight, it's not going to work, plain and simple.

Part of my challenge was that some folks try to take God out of the equation. At the same time, I didn't understand that we already name money all sorts of things all the time every day of our lives. Really, calling our financial seed whatever it is we are looking to harvest is no different from what we do every day in the marketplace.

Also, I now understand how God is glorified by answering my prayers. The more specific those prayers are, the more He gets glorified when He answers.

I tell you what. That right there gives me boldness to get very specific in how I pray. In reality, it's His reputation on the line, not mine.

On top of that, we have the power of God's promises. I didn't make the promises. He put them in His word. All I'm doing is having the

155

audacity to believe them.

That's something which is very important to emphasize here. It is critical that your faith be anchored in the right place. This means your faith must be placed in God, on His word and His promises that we find in scripture, not on the process itself.

We must stay in relationship with God and look to Him with all our giving. If we look at our giving as some sort of transaction, or just go through the motions like we are paying a bill, then we are going to see very inconsistent and unproductive results.

Every bit of this goes back to God. It's nothing more than the way He laid it out in His word. His ways are higher than our ways. When we line up with God's ways, we will see God results.

I'm just silly enough to believe what He said and do it. He's the one who gets credit for the results.

> *Teach me Your way, O Lord;*
> *I will walk in Your truth;*
> *Unite my heart to fear Your name.* — Psalms 86:11 (NKJV)

Before I share some testimonies, let's review Seed Planting and Harvesting.

What is seed planting? Money given in order to receive a specific harvest.

Who is it given to? The ministry or Kingdom purpose that God Himself tells us.

Motivation: Faith and Reward.

Promise: Thirty, sixty, hundredfold return on what was given.

Key Scripture: Mark 4:8

> *But other seed fell on good ground and yielded a crop that sprang up, increased and produced: some thirtyfold, some sixty, and some a hundred.*

Personal Examples

One of the big questions I like to try and answer is, "What does that look like?" So let's look at some practical examples of times when Lisa and I sowed financial seeds, and let me share the results we saw.

Ministry Financial Partners

One of the first things we sowed financial seed for, once we were sure God was calling us overseas as missionaries, was more income for our own ministry. I mean really, this was the whole reason Lisa and I started searching the scriptures for God's ways in the areas of our finances in the first place.

As we dug into this, Lisa and I felt God was impressing on us to sow a financial seed for increase in our financial partnership to our ministry. We figured out how much partnership we needed to live in Scotland. That amount was the harvest we were looking to receive.

Next we prayerfully took that harvest to God and asked Him how much seed we should sow and what ministry we should sow it into.

Once we came into unity on what we heard from God, we gave that amount as a seed for the specific harvest of increased partnership to cover what we needed to live here in Scotland. Interestingly, we can look back at a graph of the income into our ministry and see that it increased dramatically from that point up to the level we needed to be here.

The only thing we did differently was sow that seed, and believe we received the promise of that harvest.

In that case we were sowing money and also harvesting money. But what about sowing for things other than money?

House In Scotland

We've already talked about our house here in Dumfries. If you remember, months before we moved here Lisa and I put together a list of what we wanted to see in our Scottish house. We came up with 28 items on that list.

We were very specific in what we prayed to God to receive in our house.

At the same time we also wanted something to lock our faith into as we believed for the house God had for us here in Scotland. So we prayed over that list and asked God about sowing seed towards harvesting that house to live in once we got to Scotland.

Lisa and I agreed on an amount we thought God was saying, and on the ministry where He would have us sow that seed, and we did.

Do you remember how many houses we looked at when we got to Dumfries?

Two.

We got off the train in Lockerbie on a Thursday and stayed with some friends. We were able to get an appointment to look at a house on Friday. It was a nice enough house. But it really only hit about half the things on our list.

Lisa had been scouring the internet sites like Gumtree for months looking at potential places to rent. Dumfries is not a big city. So as you can imagine, there wasn't a massive selection to choose from here.

Then on Saturday morning a new listing showed up that looked promising. The earliest appointment we could get to look at that one was Monday evening.

As you know, that second house ticked nearly everything on our list from the get-go. And a year after we moved in, we got the last item we put on that list for our house. 28 of 28, 100% of everything we believed for!

But here's the bit I find most interesting. Someone else was lined up to rent that house. They backed out on Thursday. The exact same day we stepped off the train in Lockerbie and formally arrived in Scotland.

God saved that house especially for us. He had someone keep it off the market until the exact moment we were ready for it. It was two weeks to the day from when we arrived here in Scotland until we were able to move into the house. I'm told that's pretty quick here.

Facility for the Bible College

Let's talk about the building we we meet in for the Bible college here in Dumfries. Three years before we arrived in Scotland, when we first heard the call from God to start this new endeavor, Lisa went online to see what kinds of spaces might be available to rent. She found the very building that we are in, Kindar House on the Crichton Campus, was available.

When we had to write a full ministry plan for how we intended to go about getting this location up and running, we had to include information about costs for property. This building was one of the places we used to base our figures on.

Well, we saw how well it worked when we got specific with our house and sowed a financial seed for that. So Lisa and I made a list of things we thought we needed in the school here.

Then we got with God in prayer to see how much seed we should sow and where we should sow it for a facility that matched what was on our list. We sowed that financial seed and believed for the facility we now meet in.

Now here we are.

And we got our space to rent without a whole lot of stress and drama too.

I went back and reviewed our list recently. We had twenty-three items on it. The space we ended up in has everything we were believing for except for half of one item.

The second thing on our list was "Good amount of light with double pane windows." In Scotland they call that "double glazing" for the windows. We've got the light. There's plenty of that. But, because the building is registered as a historic structure, or what they call here a listed building, they are single pane windows.

Basically because our building is more than 125 years old, there are restrictions on what they can do to improve it. That makes it hard to change out the windows with more energy efficient ones.

All that to say, we're thrilled to be located in the wonderful facility we have.

Lisa's Second Driving Test

Getting licensed to drive in the UK was one of the bigger stressors of transitioning to life in Scotland for Lisa and me. We were allowed to drive for the first year on our American driver's licenses. But the law requires us to have a UK driving licence once we were resident here for more than a year. (They even have a different spelling for the credential here!)

The fact that we've both been driving with really good driving records for well over thirty years didn't count for anything. Plus, the testing process here is much more rigorous than it was for us back in the States.

Neither of us passed our first practical driving tests.

Keep in mind that we knew well in advance how challenging the UK driving test is. We did our part in the natural by taking numerous driving lessons with an excellent driving instructor. So it's not like we took the test for granted by any means.

Anyway, after Lisa did not pass her first test, she felt led to sow a financial seed for a passing score on her second test. She got with God and to find out the measure she needed to sow, along with where to sow it.

She sowed that seed in faith and she passed her second test, no problem.

I, on the other hand, did not see a need to sow a seed for my second test. I'd never failed the same test twice in my life. So it never entered my thinking that I might not pass the second time around. But guess what? I did not pass my second test either.

Then I got stupid. I won't go into all the painful details, but the short version is I decided to copy Lisa and sow a financial seed to get a test cancelation appointment so I could retest before the time I was allowed to drive on my American license expired.

But to be perfectly honest, I didn't sow that seed in faith. I was sowing in fear trying to "make" something happen. I didn't want to look bad and be without a license for a few weeks.

In the end, I needed to wait nearly a month before I was able to retest. I generally do the overwhelming majority of the driving because I genuinely enjoy driving, and I'm an excellent driver (even according to our driving instructor.)

Yet I still had an opportunity to enjoy the humility of a few weeks when I was not legally allowed to drive. Fortunately, Lisa is also an excellent driver. So it was good for me to enjoy the passenger seat for a bit.

I share that failure on my part to remind you that this is not a formula. This is not a way to manipulate God. We cannot be operating in fear and expect to see Kingdom results. It only works when we operate in faith. Pretending you're in faith when you really aren't, like I did, doesn't work.

I never really got a word from God about where or how much to sow. I was rushed, so I pressed ahead with my best guess instead of waiting to hear from Him. Needless to say, I don't recommend that approach.

Let that be an encouragement for you. Just because we don't get it exactly right every time doesn't mean that we shouldn't keep stepping out in faith. Keep stepping out. For in due season you will reap, if you do not lose heart.

Our Visas!!

You can trust me on this. I know sowing financial seed for a specific harvest works. Let me tell you the story of our visas.

As Americans, Lisa and I need to have a visa from the British Government to be able to work here legally. So for us, the visa was a hard requirement to get here to open the school.

We could not initiate that entirely from the States. Work visas must be sponsored by a local organization approved by the British Government as a sponsoring agency. So the decision was made that the ministry here in the UK that oversees the UK Bible college locations would go through the rather involved and expensive process to get approved by the Home Office as a sponsoring agency.

The plan was, that once they received approval as a sponsoring agency, they would then issue us a sponsoring certificate so we could apply for our visas.

The ministry chose to hire a consulting firm to help walk them through the sponsoring agency application process because they felt it was complicated enough and important enough to make sure they did things the right way the first time.

On the 18th of August (a Thursday), they submitted the full sponsoring agency application packet to the Home Office. The consulting firm said that the ministry should hear something back somewhere between the first of September and the middle of October.

So we prepared ourselves to wait a bit on that.

You can imagine our excitement when I saw the email come across on the 8th of September that the Home Office had approved the ministry to be a sponsoring agency. The consulting firm said that was the electronic approval and that they needed some information from a physical letter that would be posted to the ministry from the Home Office. They told me once they had that info they could initiate the sponsoring certificate so Lisa and I could apply for our visas.

The sponsoring agency approval process was the big variable in our timeline. That part was a six week window. So getting that approval was our trigger to start the final preparations to leave the States. Everyone involved expected everything else to happen fairly quickly after that.

We had arranged for someone to move into our house. That person was going to take over ownership of our cat. There was a lot of logistics to coordinate.

However two weeks went by and we didn't hear anything. So I sent an email asking what was up. The ministry and the consulting firm said they were working on it and they would get back with me.

I'm thinking, how long does it take for a letter to go from somewhere in London to central England?

Anyway, on Tuesday of the next week Lisa felt she heard God give her the word "logjam". She took that to mean there was a logjam with our visa process. She thought we should sow a financial seed to break that logjam.

That sounded like a good idea to me so we agreed to pray about where to sow and how much we should give as our seed.

On Thursday we talked about it again. Interestingly enough the ministry back in the Colorado where we were waiting was having a "Sower Seminar" for their own partners that next weekend. Since Lisa and I partner with them, we planned on attending that event. We knew they were bringing in a special guest speaker for the seminar that Saturday.

I felt God was saying the offering that was received at that guest speaker's session was the offering to sow our seed into. Lisa agreed with that.

At that point I was still not hearing as clearly as Lisa on how much to sow, and I didn't have any idea what God was saying on the amount. I suggested we should keep praying about it.

But then we forgot to talk about it again.

All of a sudden we found ourselves in that meeting and they were getting ready to receive an offering. We were sitting with a group of friends, and there was someone sitting between me and Lisa. So we couldn't discuss it.

Lisa texted me to ask how much to sow into that offering. I gave her a figure. She replied with double that amount. Since that seemed like a better number to me, we sowed her larger amount.

Then she texted me exactly the harvest we were believing for from that seed, to be sure we were in agreement. This is what she said:

"We are seeding this for a breakthrough in the ministry receiving the proper paperwork, certificate and then our approved visas" (I went back later and took a screenshot of our conversation.)

We sowed that seed in that offering and had total peace the issue was resolved. That was Saturday, October 1st.

We had house guests because it was the week of the local Ministers Conference there in Colorado. Plus, with the conference on, we were connecting with a ton of people that we hadn't seen in a while.

It wasn't until the following Saturday after everyone left that I had this powerful urging to email and find out what the blazes was going on with the visa process. But I knew folks would be out of the office over the weekend and I wanted my email to be at the top of their inbox when they came in Monday morning.

So Sunday night before I went to bed I sent an email asking what's up. If there was a problem Lisa and I would need to start looking into different arrangements because someone was moving into our house at the end of October.

When I got up Monday morning there was an email waiting on me. The gist of it was, "Praise God! We're moving forward again!"

Lisa and I were thinking, "what do you mean *again*"? We didn't know we weren't moving forward.

Here's what happened that we didn't know about. The British Home Office approved the ministry to be a sponsoring agency. But they did not allocate them any visas to sponsor. That's kind of useless.

In the fifty or so years that the consulting firm had been doing this kind of work, they had never seen that happen before. So they assumed it was a mistake and asked the Home Office to correct it.

Then there were a bunch of back and forth emails between the consulting firm, the ministry, and the Home Office.

Finally on September 27th the Home Office sent an email. The gist of it was that they'd reviewed what they'd done and it was perfectly legal. Therefore they would consider the request for review through their normal appeals process. The ministry should expect to hear a final determination in *18 weeks!*

That meant waiting another four and a half months!!

It was also the exact same day that Lisa heard God say, "logjam". We sowed our seed the following Saturday.

The Saturday after that, the one where I felt an urgency to send my email asking what's up, the ministry received yet another email from the Home Office. The gist of that one was, "Never mind. Here's your allocation."

The consulting firm had never seen *that* happen before either!

Later, we told this story to one of our classmates and she asked us why we didn't just pray and exercise our authority to resolve the problem. That's a good question.

I had to take that to God and ask Him. Why not just exercise my authority as a believer in that?

Here's what He showed me. I don't have any authority over the British Government. I cannot make the British Government do anything it doesn't want to do.

However, I do have access to someone who does have authority over all governments. Isaiah 9:6 says the government will be upon His shoulder.

Then, in Romans 13:1 Paul tells us this:

> Let every soul be subject to the governing authorities. For there is no authority except from God, and the authorities that exist are appointed by God.

If all governmental authorities are appointed by God Himself, then He has authority over them. And God put in place a way that we can give Him the legal right to move governments on our behalf through sowing seed for a specific harvest.

Remember, the reason we needed the government to act in our favor with the visas was to make it possible for us to step into the assignment God gave us.

From the moment the logjam broke until we got into our house here in Scotland things fell into place, click, click, click.

We applied for our visas and had them back in hand within 48 hours. On the first Monday in November we flew to Virginia to spend some time with my parents before we left the country. The next day was election day, when Trump won the election. That Thursday we completed the sale of our house in Savannah Georgia remotely from my parents house in Virginia. Then the next day we were on a plane moving to the UK.

Once we won the victory with our visas the rest of it came together incredibly smoothly.

I can't tell you the details of how every little bit of this works any better than I can tell you everything about how electricity works. I just know that when I go over to the wall and flick the switch the lights should come on. If they don't, then there's a problem and I need to get some help.

And who gets the glory in this? Certainly not Chris and Lisa. We had no idea what was going on with the government over in the UK.

It was God who gave Lisa the word logjam. He was the one who told us what field to sow in and how much seed to plant. And then God was the one who shook the British Government enough that someone in the Home Office sent an email on a Saturday. I mean what government bureaucrat anywhere in the world is sending work emails on a Saturday?

Sowing financial seed the way I've talked about works. I've seen it enough to know that it does. And when it doesn't, like when I tried to force an earlier driving retest, I go to God to find out why.

In that case the problem was all me. I was operating in fear instead of faith. That doesn't work at all in the Kingdom of God. The issue there wasn't a problem with planting and harvesting. That was an issue with Chris' heart.

Once I got my heart sorted out I passed my test with flying colors, no worries.

Chapter 9

Next Steps

"But don't just listen to God's word. You must do what it says. Otherwise,
you are only fooling yourselves."
— James 1:22 (NLT)

Your Choice

We have covered a lot of ground in this book and you've been given a fair amount of information to process. You now know the difference between the Kingdom of God and the world's cursed mammon system. Hopefully you see the power of God's promises and how He is glorified by answering our prayers so you can grow in boldness to step out and pray very specific prayers.

I've also presented several different ways that God put in place for us to both give generously and prosper too in His Kingdom.

What you choose to do next is important.

If you set this book down and think you'll do something with this information someday in the future, then it's very likely you won't ever get around to it. Then nothing will change for you.

Choosing to put your faith to work will require you to take some sort of action. Like James said, *"faith without works is dead"* (James 2:26). Unless there is action on your part, your faith won't be released to see God's Kingdom work in this area of your life.

Remember these words of Jesus,

> Do not fear, little flock, for it is your Father's good pleasure to give you the kingdom. — Luke 12:32 (NKJV)

Giving as a path to increase is not natural. It's supernatural. Therefore, it's not unusual to have some fear rise up when we first step into God's ways and take action. If some of that fear comes at you, remember this. God is looking forward to giving you His Kingdom in all its fullness.

Personally I think the best place to start exercising your faith is by tithing to your local church. If you are not tithing now, or if you have been tithing without seeing any results because you were not tithing in faith, you can make that change today.

This morning, as I type this, Lisa and I gave a tithe to our local church. In our situation right now it is simpler for us to give our tithes electronically. This is what we prayed as we gave our tithe this morning, *"Lord, we thank you that you promise to open the floodgates of heaven and pour out such a blessing that it becomes a problem for us to know what to do with it all, and that you promise to rebuke the devourer for our sakes because we put you first in our finances through our tithe."*

It's nothing fancy. We just stand on God's promise to us in Malachi 3:10-11 and know that this promise is for us because we meet God's condition with our tithe.

The key is to always place your faith in God's word. Testimonies are good for encouragement. But our faith must be anchored in God's word because that's where the power of truth is found. This applies to every promise we believe God to make real in our lives.

From my perspective, the tithe is the place to start because that promise closes off access to our finances from the enemy so he can't drain off the provision God supplies to us. Once we close the back door so that the enemy cannot drain off our finances, then we can maximize the results from the other types of giving knowing God will rebuke the devourer and protect the increase we receive.

Regardless of whether you start with the tithe or one of the other ways of giving, the important part is that you choose to take action. When you put your faith in God's word to work, you will see results, which will build your faith so you can do more. This creates a virtuous cycle of *faith* —> *action* —> *results* —> *more faith* —> *more action* —> *more results,* and so on.

This is when the Kingdom of God gets really exciting!

You have the power to choose what you do next. Choose wisely.

Continue to Grow

There is always room for us to grow and we will do well to remember to continue to grow in the ways of the Kingdom. This includes both growing in faith and growing in generosity.

This does not mean that we become discontent or covet more stuff. Contentment and a desire to continue growing in the ways of the Kingdom are not contradictory. Paul speaks to this very issue toward the end of Philippians.

As he's closing his letter in Philippians chapter 4, Paul explains that he has learned to be content in all things. We can share in this contentment which results from living in God's Kingdom, trusting His abundance as our source of provision knowing God provides for every need we have. We can indeed do all things through Christ who is the very source of our strength.

Yet Paul goes on to encourage them to give to him anyway, but not because he even needs their donations. Instead, Paul's desire is to see them continue to grow in their generosity and have more fruit added to their heavenly account as a result.

There is a difference between contentment and complacency. I know this from personal experience.

In the world's cursed mammon system the goal is to acquire enough stuff to be able to finally rest. The world works for the weekend and for the day when they can finally retire and rest. Then they can do the things they really long to do.

Yet the book of Hebrews shows us a different way. In Christ, that rest we crave is already available for us. Now it's up to us to enter into it.

> *There remains therefore a rest for the people of God. For he who has entered His rest has himself also ceased from his works as God did from His. Let us therefore be diligent to enter that rest, lest anyone fall according to the same example of disobedience.* — Hebrews 4:9-11 (NKJV)

We could take an entire book to explore the rest that is now available to us in Christ. But what I'm getting at is that we no longer rely on the stuff we possess to allow us to rest and be content. Instead we rest in the finished work of Christ and draw our contentment from there.

The rest problem has already been solved for us. Now we can disconnect that desire from however much stuff we do or don't have.

Even so, we will do well to avoid falling into complacency. Lisa and I made this mistake when we arrived on the mission field.

We received enough provision to get to our assignment in Scotland, and then backed off in this area and slipped into complacency. To be fair, we had a lot going on as we got ourselves established in a new country.

In truth, we still had some worldly ways of thinking about our provision. Once we got our needs met and were satisfied, we stopped exercising our faith for increase, and therefore stopped growing in this area.

However, we discovered that God is more interested in our growth than He is in us reaching a particular destination. Like Paul, God's desire is for us to continue to grow in our generosity and have more fruit added to our heavenly account. We should never stop growing.

Not only that, but we discovered that God also desires for each of us to continue to expand our influence for His Kingdom in our area of assignment. That means our assignments grow because God has more people and more lives for us to impact in positive ways.

Bigger assignments require more provision. Complacency shuts off the growth we must experience to move into those bigger assignments from God. If we attempt to rationalize our complacency by pretending it's really contentment, we deceive ourselves.

Therefore I encourage you to keep growing in this area. Provision will fuel your vision. As God expands your vision, you will need to dig even deeper into these truths so you can see more provision come into your life to allow you to turn that vision into reality. You will likely need to revisit them regularly as you stretch your faith to believe for the growth that moves you into those larger assignments.

As I have been writing this book, Lisa and I have been shaken out of our own complacency, and we are growing in this area again, praise God!

Personally, we long to have the ability and provision so we can always give every time the desire strikes us. We're not there yet. But we are growing again. I encourage you to do the same.

Get in Touch

If you would like to get in touch with us at NewCREEations Ministries to ask questions, or share a testimony of God's goodness, the best two ways to reach us are through our website and our Facebook page.

Our website is found here,
NewCREEations.org

Our Facebook page is found here,
facebook.com/NewCREEations

One resource that I would like to mention is our Daily Reflections email devotional that our ministry partners help us provide absolutely free of charge. We appreciate that you are likely very busy. That's why we keep our devotionals short so that you can read them in about a minute.

It's a quick, daily dose of encouragement delivered right to your email inbox every morning. We get positive feedback every month from subscribers who are blessed by our devotionals. It's our prayer that it will be a blessing for you too.

You can subscribe to our Daily Reflections on our website here, NewCREEations.org/daily-reflections

I pray that everything you put your hand to is blessed by God beyond your wildest expectations!

Made in the USA
Middletown, DE
01 June 2020